Memoir of
RICHARD SIBBES

The Life of Richard Sibbes

by
Alexander B. Grosart

BENEDICTION CLASSICS

ISBN: 978-1-78943-075-2.
© 2019 Benediction Classics, Oxford

"God knows we have nothing of ourselves,
therefore in the covenant of grace,
He requires no more than He gives,
but gives what He requires,
and accepts what He gives."

"See a flame in a spark, a tree in a seed.
See great things in little beginnings."

MEMOIR OF RICHARD SIBBES, D.D.

CHAPTER I.

'MEMORIALS' THAT MIGHT HAVE BEEN.

Izaak Walton—Dr William Gouge—Richard Baxter—John Davenport, B.D.—
Leading ' Puritans '—Sibbes's own indifference.

THERE are more than common reasons to cause regret that hitherto there has not been, and in this later time can scarcely be, a worthy life of the '*heavenly*' RICHARD SIBBES (the adjective, like the 'venerable' Bede, the 'judicious' Hooker, the 'holy' Baxter, being the almost invariable epithet associated with every mention of his name, through many generations after his departure).* I look upon my own gatherings, after no small expenditure of time and endeavour, all the more sorrowfully because of these reasons. I would fain have placed upon the honoured forehead of the author of the 'Bruised Reed' and 'Soul's Conflict' a wreath of ' amaranthine flowers ;' but alas ! have instead with difficulty gleaned a few crushed and withered leaves, some poor spires of faded grass and braids of grave-stone moss, with perchance a sprig of not altogether scentless thyme ; whereas in the course of my researches, I have come upon various notices and scintillations of revelation, which shew how different it might have been had contemporaries discharged their duty. These tantalizing indications

---

* 'Heavenly.' The famous Dr Manton thus speaks of him : ' This is mentioned . . . . because of that excellent and peculiar gift which the worthy and reverend author had in unfolding and applying the great mysteries of the gospel in a sweet and mellifluous way ; and, therefore, was by his hearers usually termed the "sweet dropper"—sweet and heavenly distillations usually dropping from him with such a native elegancy, as is not easily to be imitated.'—(To the Reader . . . . Commentary . . . . on 2 Cor. i.). ' That " heavenly " man,' says Zachary Catlin ; and Neal, ' His works discover him to have been of a " heavenly," evangelical spirit.'—(Hist. of the Puritans, vol. i. 582, edition, 3 vols. 8vo, 1837.)

of personal knowledge, and ot reserved and now lost information, may perhaps most fitly introduce our narrative.

First of all, in that 'Last Will and Testament,' over which so many eyes have brimmed with unsorrowing tears—drawn out ' in a full age,' very shortly before the venerable writer went up to lay his silver crown of gray hairs at His feet—good, gentle, blithely garrulous Izaak Walton bequeaths, among numerous other tokens and legacies, his copies of the ' Bruised Reed' and 'Soul's Conflict,' and there gleams upon the antique deed, like a ray of sunlight, these noteworthy words about them :--' To my son Izaak, I give Doctor Sibbes his Soul's Conflict, and to my daughter his Bruised Reed, DESIRING THEM TO READ THEM SO AS TO BE WELL ACQUAINTED WITH THEM.'* Nor was this the only expression of esteem for Sibbes by the ' old man eloquent.' In a copy of ' The Returning Backslider,' now preserved in Salisbury Cathedral library, he has written this inscription :—

' Of this blest man, let this just praise be given, .
Heaven was in him, before he was in heaven.—IZAAK WALTON.'

Pity that either Wotton was not assigned to another, or that Richard Sibbes made not a sixth to the golden five 'Lives' of this most quaintly-wise and wisely-quaint of all our early English biographers. How lovingly, how tenderly, with salt of wit and warbling of poetic prose, would he have made ' sacrifice to the memory' (his own phrase) of Master Richard Sibbes, the more than equal of Donne or Herbert, Sanderson or Wotton, and only in degree, not in kind, beneath Hooker himself.

Again, in Sibbes's own will, the usual sum was left to Dr William Gouge of ' Blackfryer's, London,' to preach a funeral sermon. The wording runs, ' To my reverend frende Dr Gouge, I doe give as a testimony of my love, twenty shillings, desiring him to take the paynes to preach my funeral sermon.' Pity once more that this noble preacher, whose great ' Exposition of Hebrews ' is worthy of a place beside the kindredly-massive folios of John Owen, having preached it, as he doubtless did, gave not his ' sermon' to the press. Spoken by one who was his fellow-student at the university, and who knew and greatly loved him, while men's eyes were yet wet for him, while the tones of his 'sweet-dropping' voice (Manton's word) still lingered in the groined roof of the chapel of Gray's Inn, it must have contained not a little that we of the nineteenth century would have prized. It is vexatious that importunity should have got printed this large-thoughted man's

* ' Will of Walton.' Introductory Essay to ' The Angler' by Major, 4th edition, 1844, pp. xlii.-vi.

6

funeral sermons, for a ' Mrs Margaret Ducke !' and numerous others equally unknown, and secured not this.

Further, Richard Baxter, his survivor for upwards of half a century, might have been the biographer of Sibbes. In the story of his earlier days, in that marvellous ' Reliquiæ Baxterianæ,' which won the heart of Coleridge, he speaks gratefully of him :—' About that time [his fifteenth year] it pleased God that a poor pedlar came to the door that had ballads and some good books, and my father bought of him Dr Sibbes's Bruised Reed. This also I read, and found it suited my state and seasonably sent me, which opened more the love of God to me, and gave me a livelier apprehension of the mystery of redemption, and how much I was beholden to Jesus Christ.'* This circumstance alone, observes Granger, in his meagre and chary fashion missing the right word ' immortal,' would have rendered his (Sibbes's) name memorable.'† How priceless would have been a life of Sibbes from this like-minded man, as a companion to his Alleine ! How thankfully should we have spared half a dozen of his ' painful' controversial books for half a dozen pages of such a memoir !

Nor is my roll of casualties—shall I say ?—done. In the address ' to the Christian Reader,' prefixed to ' The knowledge of Christ indispensably required of all men who would be saved' (4to, 1653), of JOHN DAVENPORT, who, like Gouge, was Sibbes's contemporary, coadjutor, and bosom friend, he informs us of a grievous loss to himself and to us :—' My far distance from the press,' he says, dating from his sequestered ' study in Newhaven,' New England, ' and the hazards of so long a voyage by sea, had almost discouraged me from transmitting this copy ; foreseeing that whatsoever σφαλματα‡ are committed by the printer, men disaffected will impute it to the author ; and being sensible of my great loss of some manuscripts by a wreck at sea, together WITH THE LIVES OF SUNDRY PRECIOUS ONES, about six years since.' From the peculiarly close and endeared friendship between the two, there can be little doubt that among those precious ones would be Richard Sibbes.

Then again, we have Thomas Goodwin, Thomas Manton, and Philip Nye, Simeon Ash, and Jeremiah Burroughs, John Sedgwick, Arthur Jackson, James Nalton, and John Dod, John Hill, John Goodwin, Robert Towne, Joseph Church, Lazarus Seaman, William Taylor, Ezekiel Culverwell, in truth, all the foremost puritan names of the period, as the writers of ' Prefaces,' ' Epistles,' ' Dedications.'

* ' Baxter,' R. B., pp. 8, 4, lib. i., pt. 1, 1696, folio.
† ' Granger,' Biog. Hist. of England, 2d edition, 1776.
‡ That is, ' slips, blunders.'

addresses 'To the Reader,' in the original quartos and duodecimos as they were issued in quick succession. In these there are provoking hints, so to speak, of withheld information. Thus say Ash, Nalton, and Church : 'The scope and business of this epistle is not so much to commend the workman (whose name is a sweet savour to the church), as to give a short and summary view of the generals handled in this treatise. THOUGH MUCH MIGHT BE SAID of this eminent saint, if either detraction had fastened her venomous nails in his precious name, or the testimony of the subscribers of this epistle might give the book a freer admission into thy hands.'*
Again, John Goodwin thus pleads : 'Good reader, to discourse the worth or commendations of the author, especially the pens of others having done sacrifice unto him in that kind, *I judge it but an unpertinency*, and make no question but that if I should exchange thoughts or judgments with thee herein, *I should have but mine own again.*† A sketch of our saintly Calvinist by the great Arminian would have been worth having.

Once more, Arthur Jackson, William Taylor, and James Nalton, deem any enlargement supererogatory : 'WE NEED SAY NOTHING OF THE AUTHOR, his former labours sufficiently 'speak for him in the gates,' his memory is HIGHLY HONOURED AMONGST THE GODLY LEARNED. He that enjoys the glory of heaven needs not the praises of men upon earth.'‡

Further, how many pleasant memories lay behind, when Jeremiah Burroughs thus poured out his reverence and love : 'Bless God for . . . . : this work, AND THE MAN THAT INDITED IT, a man, for matter always full, for notions sublime, for expression clear, for style concise—a man spiritually rational and rationally spiritual—one that seemed to see the insides of nature and grace and the world and heaven, by those perfect anatomies he hath made of them all.'§

Finally (for it were endless to cite all), in the 'Marrow of Ecclesiastical History' (folio, 1675), in the address 'to the Christian Reader,' signed 'Simeon Ash, John Wall,' we read : 'Here, *we might have given in a true though short character* of some precious servants and ministers of Christ, whose graces were admired whilst they lived, and whose memory their surviving friends do much honour, viz., Dr Preston, SIBBES, Taylor, Stoughton,' &c.

There are again and again such things, in every variety of loving

* 'To the Reader,' Heavenly Conference betwixt Christ and Mary, 12mo, 1654. 4to, 1656.
† 'To the Reader,' Exposition of 3d chapter of Philippians, &c., 4to, 1639.
‡ 'To the Reader,' Glorious Feast of the Gospel, 4to, 1650.
§ 'To the Reader,' The Christian's Portion, 12mo. 1638.

epithet, but we look in vain for any adequate memorial of the tender and tenderly treasured friendships ; for even the welcome gossip that abounds, of far inferior men.

The 'evil days and evil tongues,' the crowding and trampling of events, England's Ἰλιὰς κακῶν, that made men hold their breath and ask, 'What next?' explains, if it does not mitigate, the neglect of Sibbes's friends to place on record their knowledge and wealth of regard for him. He departed when the shadows of great calamities were falling, huge and dark, over the nation—calamities that were to recall, as with a clarion-blast, John Milton from Italy ; and it is easily to be understood, how, under such circumstances, there was delay issuing in forgetfulness. To all this must be added Sibbes's own splendid indifference to any blazoning of his name or fame, other than what might come spontaneously. His three small volumes—all that were published during his own life, under his own sanction—were literally compelled from him. Of the first, the 'Bruised Reed,' he tells us, with a touch of complaint, almost of anger, ' *To prevent further inconvenience,* I was drawn to let these notes pass with some review, considering there was an *intendment of publishing them by some who had not perfectly taken them.* And these first as being next at hand.' Of the 'Soul's Conflict,' he says also, ' I began to preach on the text about twelve years since in the city, and afterwards finished the same in Gray's Inn. After which, *some having gotten imperfect notes, endeavoured to publish them without my privity.* Therefore, to do *myself right, I thought fit to reduce them to this form.'*

All this was the expression, not of passing irritation, much less of petulancy wearing the vizard of modesty, but of principle. For, in his 'Description of Christ,' the introductory sermons to the 'Bruised Reed' (which are now restored to their proper place), he had deprecated all eagerness after human applause. ' Let us commit the fame and credit,' says he, ' of what we are or do to God. *He will take care of that,* let us take care to be and to do as we should, and then *for noise and report,* let it be good or ill as God will send it. . . . . *If we seek to be in the mouths of men, to dwell in the talk and speech of men,* God will abhor us. . . . . Therefore let us labour to be good *in secret.* Christians should be as minerals, rich in the depth of the earth. That which is least seen is his (the Christian's) riches. We should have our treasure deep ; for the discovery of it, we should be ready when we are called to it ; and for all other accidental things, let it fall out as God in his wisdom sees good. . . . . God will be careful enough to get us applause. . . . . As much reputation as is fit for a man will follow him in

being and doing what he should. *God will look to that.* Therefore we should not set up sails to our own meditations, that unless
we be carried with the wind of applause, to be becalmed, and not
go a whit forward, but we should be carried with the Spirit of God,
and with a holy desire to serve God and our brethren, and to do
all the good we can, and never care for the speeches of the world,
. . . . We should, from the example of Christ, labour to subdue
this infirmity, which we are sick of naturally. . . .' Then, in words
that have the ring of Bacon in them, 'We shall have glory
enough, and be known enough to devils, to angels, and men, *ere
long.* Therefore, as Christ lived a hidden life—that is, he was not
known what he was, that so he might work our salvation, so let
us be content to be hidden ones.' More grandly, and even more
like a stray sentence from 'The Essayes,' he elsewhere gives the
secret of his unconcern as to what men might say or leave unsaid
of him. 'THERE WILL BE A RESURRECTION OF CREDITS, as well as
of bodies. We'll have glory enough BY AND BY.' The very ease,
nay, negligence of that 'by and by' (recalling Henry Vaughan's
'other night,' in his superb vision of the great ring of eternity),
sets before us one who 'looked not at the things that are *seen and
temporal,* but at the things unseen and eternal,' one who would
shine not in the lower firmament of human fame, but up higher,
in the 'new heavens,' as a star for ever and ever.

With all explanations, and all the modesty of Sibbes himself,
we cannot help lamenting that his contemporaries so readily ac-
quiesced in his choice of being a 'hidden one.'

But I must now try to put together such particulars as have been
found, and in proceeding to do so it can only be needful to remind
those who have attempted similar service, of the Greek proverb—
Τοῖς σίτου 'αποροῦσι σπουδάζονται οἱ ὄροβοι—which may be freely rendered,
'Chick-peas are eagerly sought after when we lack corn.'

CHAPTER II.

PARENTAGE AND BIRTH—BIRTH-PLACE AND SCHOOLS.

Suffolk—Martyrs and 'Puritans'—Name, its various orthography—Bishop Mountagu
—'*Blue blood*'—Tennyson—Birth-place, Tostock, not Sudbury—Zachary Catlin
—The old English Village—Removal to Thurston—The 'Wheel-wright'—
School at Pakenham—Richard Brigs—The 'boy father of the man'—John
Milton—Contemporary 'boys'—Grammar-school at Bury St Edmunds—Father
begrudges 'expense'—Master Sibbes put in the 'wheel-wright's' shop—Friends
step in.

RICHARD SIBBES was a native of Suffolk, one of the great martyr
and puritan counties of England, that furnished many of the early

fugitives to Holland, a very unusual proportion of the emigrants to New England (whose lustrous names are still talismans over the Atlantic), and nearly a hundred of the 'ejected' two-thousand of 1662. The name 'Sibbes' is variously spelled. The spelling now given, and adopted in our title-page, is his own signature to his own dedications and 'epistles to the reader.' But he is frequently called Sibbs, and such is the orthography of his Will, as well as of his heirs and their descendants. There is a third variation, Sybbes or Sybesius. But it is the Latinized form, as it occurs in Richterus Redivivus.* A fourth, Sibs, is common to many of the original editions, and furnishes a side-thrust in a play upon the word to Bishop Mountagu, in his 'Appello ad Cæsarem' (1625), that over-clever 'Defence.' Even thus early Sibbes was speaking bravely out in his post at 'Gray's Inn' against the semi-popish practices of the prelates; and the venal bishop, afraid to strike openly, must needs hint dislike in this taunt, 'So .... with our Puritans, very *Sibs* unto those fathers of the society, every moderate man is bedaubed with these goodly habiliments of Arminianism, popery, and what not, unless he will be frantic with them for their holy cause.'† This may, perchance, be a mere jesting use of the word 'sib,' but the capital S and plural, and the man, seem to indicate an intended hit at our author, ever outspoken against such as the unquestionably astute but also unquestionably unscrupulous Richard Mountagu. The earliest occurrence of the name that I have met with is in a Robert Sibbes or Sybbs of Cony-Weston, Norfolk, who, in 1524, purchased Ladie's Manor, Rockland-Tofts, which again was sold by his son and heir, also a Robert, in 1594.‡ Perhaps, by further inquiries, it might be possible to connect the neighbouring Norfolk with the Suffolk Sibbeses; and, though I have searched in vain in Burke's 'Armoury,' and all through the Davy 'Suffolk MSS.,'§ for genealogical record, it is possible that further research might even shew 'blue blood' in the descent of the author of the 'Bruised Reed.' But it would serve

* 'Richterus Redivivus.' In a curious letter of Christopher Arnold, containing new and apparently unused information about Milton. Writing to Geo. Richter (from Lond., A.D. 7 Aug. (*sic*) 1651, printed in Richterus Redivivus, p. 485), he says, 'In Academia Cantabrigiensi vir peramans mei, Abrah. Whelocus, Arab. atque Anglo-saxonicæ Linguarum Professor et Bibliothecarius publicus codices manuscriptos cum primis Græcos, &c. .... Obstupui in Johannitica (bibliotheca), cum mihi magnum sacrorum librorum Græcobarbarorum copiam ostenderent, a benefactore quodam anonymo, suasione Richardi Sybbes, S. Th. Prof. et hujus Coll. quondam socii senioris, A.D. 1628, dono oblatorum.'

† 'Appello ad Cæsarem, a Just Appeale from Two Unjust Informers.' By Richard Mountagu. 4to, 1625, p. 139.

‡ Blomefield's Norfolk, vol. i., pp. 481–82. § In British Museum. Addl. MSS.

little purpose to do so, or to prove him '*sib*' to this, that, or the other great family. The far-fountained 'red' ichor that has come down from

'The grand old gardener and his wife '*

suffices, the more especially as, at the time of his birth at least, our author's family was assuredly lowly, and of the people :

'Kind hearts are more than coronets,
And simple faith than Norman blood.'†

In all preceding notices, Sudbury, the old town, so far back as Edward III.'s times inhabited by the Flemings, is given as Sibbes's birth-place. 'At Sudbury,' says Neal ('History of the Puritans'), and Brook ('Lives of the Puritans'), and so all the 'Biographical Dictionaries.' '*Nigh* Sudbury,' says Fuller; '*At the edges* of Suffolk, *near* Sudbury,' says Clarke. This is a mistake. The town, 'as great as most, and ancient as any,' according to Thomas Fuller, that can boast of Thomas Gainsborough and Thomas Constable later, as natives, and of Faithful Teate, William Jenkyn, and Samuel Peyto earlier, as ministers, can afford to give up an honour to which it has no claim. Tostock, not Sudbury, was his birth-place. The 'registers' of the period, of Sudbury and Tostock alike, have perished; but a contemporary manuscript 'Memoir' of Sibbes, from the pen of Zachary Catlin (of whom more anon), which the stream of time, while engulphing so much else of what was precious and what was worthless, has floated down and placed by lucky accident in my possession, states the fact. As this contemporary manuscript must be frequently laid under contribution in the sequel, it may be as well to give here its proem, which is sufficient, apart from what will subsequently appear, to attest its authority and trustworthiness. 'At the request of a noble friend, Sir William Spring, I have here willingly contributed to the happy memory of that worthy man of God, Dr Sibbes, a few such flowers as I could collect, either from the *certain relation of those that knew his first education, or from mine own observation of him* at that distance whereat we lived. And if anything here recorded may seem convenient for his purpose, who is (as I am informed)

---

* and † Tennyson. 'Lady Clara Vere de Vere '. Even were it possible to trace the name of Sibbes up to 'Norman blood,' we must remember our Scottish proverbs :—

A' Stuarts are no *sib* to the king,   }   = Though of the same name,
A' Campbells are no *sib* to the duke, }   not of the same family.

Moreover, as he says himself of another (Sherland), 'What should I speak of these things, when he has personal worth enough? I need not go abroad to commend this man, for there were those graces and gifts in him that made him so esteemed, that verily I think no man of his place and years lived more desired, and died more lamented.' ('Christ is Best,' page 347 of this volume of the works.)

about to publish the lives of some worthies deceased, I shall think
my labour well bestowed. For I am not of that philosopher's
mind, who lighting upon a book newly put forth, entitled, "The Encomium of Hercules," cast it away, saying, *Et quis Lacedæmoniorum
eum vituperavit?* accounting it a needless work to praise him whom
no man did or could find fault withal. I rather judge it a commendable thing to perpetuate and keep fresh the memory of such
worthy men whose examples may be of use for imitation in this
declining and degenerate age.'* I give his *ipsissima verba* of the
birth-place, as above, and embrace in the quotation the birth-date
as well. 'But I come to the matter. This Richard, the eldest son
of Paul Sibs and Johan [= Joanna?] was born at Tostock, in Suffolk,
four miles from Bury, anno domini 1577.'† The source of the
blunder of making Sudbury the birth-place is evidently confound-
ing '*Bury*' St Edmunds with Sud*bury*. Tostock is 'nigh' the
former, but not 'nigh' the latter, and cannot at all be described as
'on the edges' of Suffolk, being fifteen or twenty miles in the
interior. Tostock, to which I thus restore, if not in the popular
sense a great, at least a revered, name, and one of which any place
might be proud, remains to-day very much as we may suppose it to
have been two hundred years ago, except perhaps that 'its tide
of work has ebbed away,' and it is now wholly rural. It is a small
sequestered village in Thedwestry hundred, about, as we have seen,
four miles from Bury St Edmunds, and about thirteen miles from
Sudbury.

> 'A quaint, old, gabled place
> With Church stamped on its face.

Exactly such a 'village' as 'Our Village' has made dear to us all.
Its few picturesquely scattered houses cluster around an unenclosed
'common' (once abundant in 'merry England,' but now sparse),
and present fine specimens of what every year is seeing disappear
—the peaked-roofed, mossy-thatched, or saffron-tiled 'homes' of our
forefathers of the 16th and 17th centuries, with every 'coign of van-
tage' of the over-hanging upper storeys and lozenge-paned windows,

> 'Held by old swallows on a lease of love
> Unbroken, immemorial;'

and little gardens a-front flinging out into the air the breath of

---

* Above and throughout I modernise the orthography; but in Appendix A to
this Memoir I reprint from my MS. the whole very interesting document. Thither
I refer for further information concerning its author.

† Neal gives 1579, and is followed by others; but the misprint is corrected by the
statement that his death took place in 1635, in his 57th year, which, however, ought
to be 58th. The 'Registers' of Tostock that remain commence long subsequent to
1577, and hence the date of his birth-*day* is lost.

old-fashioned flowers. It is pleasant in our day to come upon
such a virgin spot.

> 'For it is well, amid the whirr
> Of restless wheels and busy stir,
> To find a quiet spot where live
> Fond, pious thoughts conservative,
> That ring to an old chime,
> And bear the moss of time.
>
> . . . .
>
> 'And sweeter far and grander too
> The ancient civilisation grew,
> With holy war and busy work
> Beneath the spire and round the kirk
> Than miles of brick and stone
> In godless monotone.'

The 'church,' lichened and lady-ferned, but in excellent preservation, is approached by a fragrant lane that strikes off from
'the rectory,'

> ' . . . where the budding purple rose,
> Prolific of its gifts, the long year through
> Breaks into beauty.

It is dedicated to St Andrew.

> 'Nor gargoyle lacks, grotesque and quaint,
> Nor saintly niche without its saint,
> Nor buttress lightsome, nor the tower,
> Where the bell marks the passing hour,
> And peals out with our mirth,
> And tolls our earth to earth.'

The 'font'—from which no doubt little Richard Sibbes was baptized—is noticeable. The 'benches' are of dark oak, grotesquely
carved. The graves around are ozier-woven, and on some of the
stones, the once great Suffolk name of Bacon, is still to be read ;
also in the wrecks of the 'Registers' that remain, the mighty
name of Wolsey occurs, as elsewhere in the neighbourhood (by a
strange link with Germany and the Reformation), is to be found
that of Luther. We visited the primitive hamlet on one of
the finest of English September days, and our Scottish eye and
heart were touched with the quiet English scenery, long familiar
by the 'landscapes' of Suffolk's Gainsborough and Constable, and
her poets, Bloomfield and Crabbe. There were the 'Cart on a
Road,' 'Cows crossing a Ford,' 'Boys a-straddle on a Gate,' the
'Stile,' ringed with honey-suckle, and now the glowing, and now
the bleak originals of 'The Farmer's Boy' and of 'The Borough.'
Tostock was a cheery, sunny, many-memoried birth-place ; to
this hour, with its sister-villages, possessing traditions of martyrs
and reformers, Rowland Taylor and Yeoman, and, farther off,

Hooper and Coverdale and John Rogers, and legends of the Tudors and the Commonwealth. For a 'Puritan' none could have been more fitting, for all around were the family seats of grand old Puritan worthies, Barton-Mere, Talmach Hall, Pakenham, Nether Hall, where 'godly ministers' were ever welcome to the Barnardistons and Brights, Veres and Brooks, Winthrops and Riches, Springs and Cavendishes, and the Bacon stock.

But Sibbes was very soon removed thence to Thurston, a similar hamlet only about three miles distant. Here, our old worthy the Vicar of Thurston informs us, Mr and Mrs Sibbes 'lived in honest repute, brought up and married divers children, purchased some houses and lands, and there both deceased.'

There will be something to say afterward of these 'divers children' who were 'married;' but it is to be regretted that, the 'registers having perished, no positive light can be cast on the dates of the decease of the elder folks, except that the father was dead before 1608. Concerning him this is Catlin's testimony : ' His father was by his trade a wheel-wright, a skilful and painful workman, and a good, sound-hearted Christian.' ' Skilful and painful'* were very weighty words then, particularly ' painful,' which was the highest praise that could be given to a laborious, faithful, evangelical minister of the gospel. It is found in many an olden title-page, and underneath many a grave, worn face. A ' mill-wright,' or ' wheel-wright,' for they are interchangeable, was by no means an unimportant ' craftsman' in those days. In country places, such as Thurston and Tostock, where division of labour could not be carried so far as in the large towns, the ' wheel-wright' was compelled to draw largely upon his own resources, and to devise expedients to meet pressing emergencies as they arose. Necessarily this made him dexterous, expert, and ' skilful' in mechanical arrangements. If thus early, the whole of Smiles's description, on whose authority I am writing this,† does not hold (for he speaks of him devising steam-engines, pumps, cranes, and the like) ; yet in those primitive days, perhaps more than some generations later, such tradesmen were, in all cases of difficulty, resorted to, and looked upon as a very important class of workmen ; while the nature of their business tended to make them thoughtful, decided, self-reliant. The cradle of little Richard, therefore, would seem to have been rocked at a fireside not altogether unprosperous. And yet there must have been in the outset somewhat of poverty and struggle, or, the elder Sibbes will need the full benefit of Catlin's character of him. For our guileless

* Painful = full of pains, *i.e.*, painstaking, laborious.
† Smiles's Life of Brindley, in Lives of the Engineers, vol. i. p. 312.

chronicler, carrying us swiftly onward, adds immediately thereafter, 'This Richard he brought up in learning at the grammar school, *though very unwillingly in regard of the charge.*' We will in charity give Master Paul Sibs, wheel-wright, the benefit of the vicar's testimony, and ascribe the ' unwillingness' to the *res angustæ domi.* Whether or not, the ' charge,' I fear, had prematurely removed the little fellow from the school to the wheel-wright's bench, but for his own bookish tastes, and the watchful interest of friends. This is explicitly affirmed in what follows. The sentence above, that tells us of the unwilling school-learning, through the ' charge,' thus continues—' had not the youth's strong inclination to his books, and well profiting therein, with some importunities of friends, prevailed so far as to continue him at school till he was fit for Cambridge.' Most truly the ' boy was father of the man.' I turn again to the Izaak Walton-like words of the Vicar of Thurston. He says—' Concerning his love to his book, and his industry in study, I cannot omit the testimony of Mr Thomas Clark, high constable, who was much of the same age, and went to school together with him at the same time, with one Mr Richard Brigs (afterward head master of the Free School at Norwich), then teaching at Pakenham church. He hath often told me that, when the boys were dismissed from school at the usual hours of eleven and five or six, and the rest would fall to their pastime, and some-times to playing the wags with him, as being harmless and meanly apparelled (for the most part in leather), it was this youth's con-stant course, as soon as he could rid himself of their unpleasing company, to take out of his pocket or satchel one book or other, and so to go reading and meditating till he came to his father's house, which was near a mile off, and so he went to school again. This was his order, also, when his father sent him to the Free School at Bury, three or four miles off, every day. Whereby the said Mr Clark did then conceive, that he would in time prove an excel-lent and able man, who of a child was of such a manly staidness, and indefatigable industry in his study.'* Milton's immortal portraiture of ' *The* Child' may be taken to describe Master Richard :—

> ' When I was yet a child, no childish play
> To me was pleasing; all my mind was set,
> Serious to learn and know, and thence to do,
> What might be public good.'—*Paradise Regained.* [B. i. 201-204.]

The ' school near Pakenham church' has long since disappeared,

* ' *Staidness*' is the very word Lord Brooke uses to describe the youthhood of Sir Philip Sidney : and indeed his whole description is reflected in the above. Cf. the Life of the renowned Sir Philip Sidney (ed. 1652), pp. 6, 7.

MEMOIR OF RICHARD SIBBES, D.D.

and no memorial whatever has been transmitted of it. The mansion of Pakenham was the seat of the Gages, whence the mother of Sir Nicholas Bacon, father of *the* Bacon, came ; and later was the residence of Sir William Spring, at whose request Catlin drew up his notice of Sibbes. Probably, we err not in tracing back the after-friendship with Sibbes to those school-boy days. One likes to picture little Master Richard in his leathern suit (not at all uncommon at the period), studiously walking day by day from Pakenham to Thurston, and home again. Nor can we avoid thinking of other ' boys,' who were then likewise ' at school,' and destined to cross one another's paths. Not a few of them will be found united in intimate friendship with the little leathern-suited pupil of Master Brigs. With others he came into conflict. They are relegated to a footnote.*

Having obtained all that he could, apparently, at the school of Master Brigs (of whom nothing has come down), little Richard, as our last citation from the vicar's manuscript has anticipated us in stating, was sent to Bury St Edmunds, to the ' Free School' there, by which must be intended the still famous ' School' founded by Edward VI. ; and we can very well understand the zest with which one so thoughtful and eager would avail himself of the advantages of such an institution. Dr Donaldson has failed to enrol Sibbes among the celebrities of the school, an omission which, it is to be hoped, will

---

* Contemporary ' boys.' The greatest of all, Master Willie Shakespeare, rising into his teens, has only very lately been tossing his auburn curls at Stratford 'school;' and, still a 'boy,' is now wooing his fair Anne Hathaway. Master Joseph Hall is playing about Bristow Park, Ashby-de-la-Zouch, under the eye of Mistress Winifred, of whom he was to write so tenderly as his more than Monica. Away in the downs of Berks, diminutive Willie Laud is playing at marbles under the acacia-walk of Reading. Master George Herbert is ruffling the humour of his stately brother, afterwards Lord Herbert of Cherbury, the ' *doubter*,' by overturning a glass of malmsey on his slashed hose and ' roses of his shoon.' In not distant Tarring, Master John Selden is already storing up in the wizard cave of memory those treasures of learning the world is one day to marvel at. Masters Phineas and Giles Fletcher are truanting in the linden glades of their father's vicarage. Masters George Wither and Francis Quarles are agog (in strange contrast with their grim scorn of such ' gaudery,' by-and-bye) over their new lace-frill. Master William Browne is chasing the butterflies in Tavistock. Masters Ussher and Hobbes are perchance busy over their A B C. Francis Beaumont and John Fletcher are still asunder. Master Massinger, tossing ha'pence under the minster of Salisbury, no vision yet of the ' Virgin Martyr,' and no shadow of the ' *stranger's* grave ' he is to fill. Moreover, as Master Sibbes was thus footing it between Thurston and Bury, men were alive who had seen martyr-faces, ' pale i' the fire.' In the words of Bourne, of a few years earlier, ' The English air was thick with sighs and curses. Great men [were] heavy-hearted at the misery which had fallen upon the land . . . . and he [may] have listened to their earnest, mournful talk. (Memoirs of Philip Sidney, by H. R. Fox Bourne, 8vo, 1862, pp. 9, 10.)

17

henceforward be supplied, for any school may boast of a name so venerable as the author of the 'Bruised Reed.' In the 'registers of the school the name of Sibbes has not been recorded. One would have been glad to know some of his schoolmates. I am not aware that history or biography has named any of them, none at any rate more distinguished than himself. The statutes and other documentary manuscripts of the school have been lost, and nothing is known of its celebrated scholars till 1610—long subsequent to Sibbes—when the list is headed by that twin-brother to Pepys, Sir Symonds D'Ewes. Only one Master is given before 1583, a Philip Mandevill. In 1583, the office was filled by a John Wright, M.A., and in 1596, by Edmund Coote, M.A., who seems to have published his 'English Schoolmaster' (hardly to be placed beside 'The Schoolmaster' of Roger Ascham, though not without merit), during his short term of office.

The earliest extant list of 'boys' is dated 1656. It is a fine glimpse of the student-boy old Catlin gives, leisurely footing from Pakenham to Thurston, and it is to be remembered he did the same to the more distant Bury. We can avouch that, in this good year Eighteen hundred and sixty-two, twenty-fourth of Queen Victoria I., few more pleasant rural roads can be found than that which now winds from Thurston to Bury. On either side are picturesque hurdle-fences tangled with purple cornel, or hedge-rows odorous with hawthorn spray. But it must have been very different in Master Richard's time. Macadam was still unborn; and even a century and half later, Arthur Young* has anything but praise for this turnpike. 'I was forced,' he tells us in reference to it, 'to move as slow in it as in any unmended lane in Wales. For ponds of liquid dirt, and a scattering of loose flints, just sufficient to lame every horse that moves near them, with the addition of cutting vile grips across the road, under the pretence of letting the water off, but without effect, altogether render at least twelve out of these sixteen miles (between Bury and Sudbury) as infamous a turnpike as ever was beheld.' Alas! for bookish, studious Master Richard, if he found his school-walk such a Slough-of-Despond.

Sent to Bury 'Free School' (visiting which I looked up at the time-stained bust of its youthful royal founder with interest for Sibbes's sake, who, perchance, practised his first Latin in spelling out the not over-elegant or accurate inscription beneath), there would, no doubt, be rapid advancement. But the 'child' had become a 'lad,' and again there was threatened interruption to his school-learning. I

---

* 'Six Weeks' Tour through the Southern Counties of England and Wales.' 2d ed. 1769. Pp. 88, 89.

find an objurgation rising to my lips against this so 'unwilling' father; but it is silenced by the recollection of the vicar's testimony: 'He was a skilful and painful workman, and a good, sound-hearted Christian.' Master Catlin, I suspect thy sweet-nurtured charity was blind to Master Paul Sibs's penuriousness! It may have been, again let us say, pressure of circumstances, many mouths to be fed, multiplied 'work' demanding another pair of hands. Still it is not altogether what we should like, to find Master Richard again hindered. 'His father,' continues our vicar, 'at length *grew weary of his expenses for books and learning,* took him from school, bought him an axe and some other tools, and set him to his own trade, to the great discontent of the youth, wnose genius wholly carried him another way.' So Master Paul Sibs proposed, but Another disposed. The lad was destined to work for his generation—and many generations—with other tools than these.

CHAPTER III.

STUDENT AND PREACHER AT CAMBRIDGE.

Leaves Bury St Edmunds for ' St John's College,' Cambridge—Greaves—Knewstub —Rushbrook—Enters as ' sub-sizar '—Jeremy Taylor *'pauper scholaris '*—Progress—Degrees—B.A. — ' Fellow ' — M.A.—' Taxer ' — B.D.—Paul Bayne — ' *Conversion* '—A 'Preacher '—Lectureship of ' Trinity,' Cambridge—Memorial— ' Hobson '—Accepts—Results—Samuel Clarke—Thomas Cawton—John Cotton —' Word in season ' to Thomas Goodwin—Prevalent ' preaching.'

Once more vigilant friends stepped in. They saw the 'youth' set utterly against the grain, at the wheel-wright's bench. 'Whereupon,' approvingly, with the faintest touch of rebuke, chronicles good Zachary Catlin : 'Mr Greaves, then minister of Thurston, and Mr Rushbrook, an attorney there, knowing the disposition and fitness of the lad, sent him, *without his father's consent,* to some of the Fellows of St John's College of their acquaintance, with their letters of recommendation; where, upon examination, he was so well approved of, that he was presently entertained as a sub-sizar, shortly after chosen scholar of the house, and at length came to be Fellow of the College, and one of the taskers of the university ; his father being hardly brought to allow him twenty nobles a year towards his maintenance in Cambridge, to which some good friends in the country, Mr Greaves, Mr Knewstub, and some others, made some addition, for a time, as need required.' I am sure all my readers will wish that we knew more of those 'good friends.' All honour to the memory of 'Mr Greaves and Mr Rushbrook.' Of ' Mr Knewstub,' the scholarly, the pious, the brave-hearted, no admirer of the Puritans needs to be informed. His is truly a historic *clarum et venerabile nomen.* His letter of recommendation to St John's College would have the greater weight, in that he was one of its greatest lights, and, subsequently, its benefactor. One is pleased, nevertheless, to learn that it was ' upon examination,' not mere ' recommendation,' the youth was received. He was then in his eighteenth year. Entered as a sub-sizar, which is even beneath a sizar, young Sibbes must have been placed at a disadvantage. Jeremy Taylor, however, was entered as '*pauper scholaris,*' lower still. That has transfigured, if not ennobled, the lowly ' sizar.' Certainly the more honour is due to those who, starting with the meanest, have won for themselves the highest places. How many who entered among the highest are forgotten, while the lapse of time only brightens the lustre of our ' sub-sizar' and the '*pauper scholaris.*'

The career of Sibbes at the university was singularly successful, and indicates in the son of the wheel-wright of Tostock and Thurston, no common energy and devotion to study. It is probable that his 'school-learning' at Pakenham and Bury St Edmunds, alike, was frequently interrupted and hindered. Nevertheless, he seems to have at once placed himself abreast of the most favoured students. The records and registers of St John's College, shew that he passed B.A. in 1598-9 ; was admitted ' Fellow' 3d April 1601, commenced M.A. in 1602, taxer (the ' tasker' of Catlin) in 1608, was elected ' College Preacher' feast of 1st March 1609, and graduated B.D. in 1610.

We must return upon these dates. When Sibbes, in 1595, proceeded to Cambridge, ' *without the consent of his father,*' but with kind words of cheer and something more from Mr Greaves, Mr Knewstub, and Mr Rushbrook, it does not appear that he had any specific intentions in regard to the future. An academic life was evidently his ambition ; but to what profession, whether divinity, law, or medicine, he was ultimately to devote himself, was probably left undetermined. An event, or more accurately, *the* one great event and ' change' in every man—his *conversion* (I like and therefore use the good old puritan, because Biblical, word), in all likelihood led him to decide to serve God in the ministry of the gospel of his Son. Paul Bayne, sometimes Baine and Baines, one of the most remarkable of the earlier '*Doctrinal* Puritans' (that name of stigma imposed by Laud), whose ' Letters,' second only to those of Samuel Rutherford, and other minor books, were long the chosen fireside reading of every puritan household, and whose 'Exposition of Ephesians' is worthy to take its place beside Rogers and Byfield on Peter, Jenkyn on Jude, Petter on Mark, Elton on Colossians and Romans, Newton on John, and their kindred folios, that lie now-a-days like so many unworked mines of gold—had succeeded Perkins as preacher at St Andrew's, Cambridge, 'and it pleased God,' says Clarke, 'to make him an instrument of the conversion of that holy and eminent servant of Christ, Dr Sibbes.' Sibbes himself is reverently reticent on the momentous matter, even in his preface to Bayne's 'Exposition of the first chapter of Ephesians' (published separately in 1618), making no allusion to it ; but it probably took place somewhere about 1602–3.* In 1602, having passed M.A., he shortly thereafter became a 'preacher.' By 1608 'he was a preacher of good note.' Where he did preach we are not informed. In his address to the reader prefixed to the 'Soul's Conflict,' he states that the 'Sermons' which compose it had been preached first of all 'about twelve years' before 'in the city,' *i.e.*, London, and afterwards at 'Gray's Inn.' I have utterly failed to come upon any memorial of this 'city' ministry ; but it is probable that it was commenced between 1602 and 1607. Elected 'College Preacher' in 1609, he must have been then well known and distinguished.

In 1610, when he had graduated B.D., another very important event happened. In that year a 'Memorial' was addressed to him, which, in so far as I can learn, appears to have been the origin of the subsequently celebrated 'Trinity Lectureship,' held since by some of the greatest names of the church. The memorial gives us

---

* 'Conversion . . . . reticent.' This is quite in accord with Sibbes's declared sentiments. I would refer the reader to ' The Description of Christ,' pp. 30, 31. There he will find not more sound than admirably expressed counsels and warnings as to the 'vainglory' of publishing abroad things too solemn to be so dealt with. I assume the responsibility of affirming, that at no period have those warnings been more demanded than the present. Every one who ' loves the Lord,' who prays and longs for the coming of ' the kingdom,' who mourns the worldliness and coldness of all sections of Christ's divided church, must rejoice in the past two years' awakening and ' revival.' I would gladly recognise the work of the Spirit of God in much that has taken place. I verily believe very many have been 'born again,' and more who were half asleep have been stirred and quickened. At the same time, it were to be unfaithful and untruthful to blink the 'evil' that has mingled with the ' good.' It becomes every reverent soul to protest against those premature declarations of ' conversions,' and publication of 'experiences' that have got so common. It is perilous to forget the Master's words, Luke xvii. 20. Paul was fourteen years a ' servant' of Christ before he made known his ineffable rapture and vision. Modern ' converts,' do not allow as many hours to expire ere their whole story is blazoned in the public prints. Surely a thing so awful and so sacred, unless in very exceptional instances, is for the ear of God alone. The Tract Societies would act wisely if they circulated by thousands as a ' Tract for the Times,' Sibbes's priceless words of ' Vainglory.'

insight into the popularity of Sibbes as a preacher.* The orthography and wording of the original are retained :—

'A Coppye of the general request of the inhabitants of oʳ p'ishe deliv'ed
to Mr Sibs, publique p'acher of the house of Cambridge.

'We whose names ar heerunderwritten, the Churchewardens and P'ishion-
ers of Trinity p'ishe in Cambridge, with the ful and fre consent of Mr Jhon
Wildbore oʳ minister, duely considering the extream straytnes & div'se
other discomodities concerning the accustomed place of yʳ exercise &
desireing as much as in vs lyeth yᵉ more publique benefit of yoʳ ministery,
doe earnestlye entreat you wold be pleesed to accept of oʳ p'ishe Churche,
which al of vs doe willinglye offer you for & concerning the exercising of
yo, ministery & awditorye at the awntient and usual daye & houre. In
witnes hereof wee have heervnto set to oʳ hands this 22th (sic) of Noveber
1610.   'JOHN WILBORE,   Minister.

              'EDWARD ALMOND, ⎫
              'THOMAS BANKES, ⎬ Churchewardens.
     (Signed also by 29 Parishioners.)

The churchwardens of the parish having kindly permitted access
to their 'Records,' I find amongst them a list of the names of the subscribers to the lectureship in the several parishes of the town, with
the amount of each person's subscription, which runs generally
13s. 4d., 10s., and 6s. 8d. per annum. Three gave £1 per annum
each, of whom one was Mr Hobson, the carrier, immortalised by
Milton, and later by Steele in the 'Spectator,' and to this day
a 'household word' in Cambridge, in kindly eccentric association with the proverb, 'Hobson's choice, that or none,' which no
one book-read will need explained. One thing is noticeable, that
a goodly number of the signatures to the memorial are with
marks +. This is of the last interest and not a little touching.
The 'common people' heard Sibbes, like his Master, 'gladly,' and
the 'straytnes of the place' hindered others. This is a sign of
change for the better in Cambridge very worthy of observation.
The old longing after that full preaching of the gospel which had
characterised the period of Perkins's seraphic yet pungent ministry,
was revived. Sibbes responded to the memorial, and immediately
it was felt that 'Trinity' had a man of mark as its 'Lecturer,' the
coequal of Bayne of St Andrew's. How those saintly servants
of the same Lord would rejoice to be fellow-helpers of each other,
the younger 'serving' with the elder, as a son with a father. The
lectureship of 'Trinity' was a complete success. Besides the
townsmen, many scholars resorted to him, whereby he became, in
the words of Clarke, a 'worthy instrument of begetting many sons

* 'Trinity Lectureship.' The 'Memorial' is given by Mr Cooper in his Annals of
Cambridge, iii. 168.

and daughters unto God, besides the edifying and building up of others.'*

We have incidental confirmations of the weighty testimony of the 'Pastor of St Bennet Fink, London.' More generally, in that curious little rarity of Puritan biography, 'The Life and Death of that Holy and Reverend man of God, Mr Thomas Cawton't (1662), we read 'He conscientiously and constantly laboured to counter-work those factors of hell, and drove a trade for God in bestirring himself to insinuate into any lad that was ingenious, and was very successful therein, to the astonishment and confusion of his opposers. Many had great cause to bless God for him, and their first acquaintance with him, for his bringing them to Dr Preston's and *Dr Sibbes, his Lectures* in those times.' More specially, Cotton Mather, the Thomas Fuller of New England, tells us of one memorable conversion through his instrumentality—John Cotton, who was in turn the 'leader to Christ' of a greater than himself, Dr Preston, and whom Oliver Cromwell himself addressed as 'my esteemed friend.'‡

It were like to rubbing off with coarse fingers the powder from a moth's wing, in any wise to change the loving and grave narrative. It is as follows :—'Hitherto we have seen the life of Mr Cotton while he was not yet alive ! Though the restraining and prevent-ing grace of God had kept him from such outbreakings of sin as defile the lives of most in the world, yet like the old man who for such a cause ordered this epitaph to be written on his grave, "Here lies an old man who lived but seven years," he reckoned himself to have been but a dead man as being "alienated from the life of God," until he had experienced that regeneration in his own soul, which was thus accomplished. The Holy Spirit of God had been at work upon his young heart, by the ministering of that reverend and renowned preacher of righteousness, Mr Perkins ; but he resisted and smothered those convictions through a vain persuasion, that if he became a godly man 'twould spoil him for being a learned one. Yea, such was the secret enmity and prejudice of an unregenerate soul against real holiness, and such the torment which our Lord's witnesses give

* Clarke, Lives of Thirty-two English Divines, 3d edition, 1677, folio, p. 143.

† 'Cawton,' p. 11.

‡ Cotton and Cromwell. The letter of the great Protector, alluded to, a very striking one, will be found in Brook's Lives of the Puritans, iii. 158–9. It is also given with characteristic annotation in Carlyle's 'Cromwell,' iii. 221–225 (3d ed. 1850). When, may I ask in a foot-note, will America give us worthy editions of the still inedited and uncollected 'Works' of John Cotton, Thomas Hooker, Daven-port, and others of their kindred ? Surely this were better than much that has been reprinted over the Atlantic.

to the consciences of the earthly-minded, that when he heard the bell toll for the funeral of Mr Perkins, his mind secretly rejoiced in his deliverance from that powerful ministry by which his conscience had been so oft beleaguered; the remembrance of which things afterwards did break his heart exceedingly! *But he was at length more effectually awakened by a sermon of Dr Sibs,* wherein was discoursed the misery of those who had only a negative righteousness, or a civil, sober, honest blamelessness before men. Mr Cotton became now very sensible of his own miserable condition before God; and the errors of those convictions did stick so fast upon him, that after no less than three years' disconsolate apprehensions under them, the grace of God made him a thoroughly renewed Christian, and filled him with a sacred joy which accompanied him into the fulness of joy for ever. For this cause, as persons truly converted unto God have a mighty and lasting affection for the instruments of their conversion, *thus Mr Cotton's veneration for Dr Sibs* was after this very particular and perpetual, and it caused him to have the picture of that great man in that part of his house where he might oftenest look upon it.'*

Various similar *memorabilia* might be here adduced from the Puritan 'Biographies' and 'Histories.' One additional 'word in season,' spoken to Dr Thomas Goodwin, may suffice. In his earlier days this celebrated divine leant to Arminianism rather than to Calvinism, and it was through Sibbes that his views were cleared, to his life-long satisfaction, on the point of Jesus Christ being the Head and Representative of his people. It is also recorded that, in familiar discourse with Goodwin, Sibbes said, 'Young man, if you ever would do good, you must preach the gospel, and the free grace of God in Christ Jesus.'† The counsel was as a ' nail in a sure place,' and no reader of Goodwin needs to be told how fully and magnificently he sets forth the 'grace' of God in Christ.

Well was it that such men as Paul Bayne and Richard Sibbes were preachers in such a place and at such a time. From contemporary accounts it is apparent, that notwithstanding the profound impression 'on the town' by Perkins, and notwithstanding that there were a few who, Mary-like, 'kept all the things' they had heard from him, 'and pondered them in their hearts,' Cambridge was sunken down, as a whole, to all its former indifferentism and formality. The preaching that was fashionable among the 'wits' of

---

* Cotton. Magnalia Christi Americana : or the Ecclesiastical History of New England, book iii., c. i., § 5, p, 15. Folio, 1702.

† Robert Trail, A.M., Justification by Faith, Works, vol. i. p. 261 (edition 4 vols, 8vo, 1810).

the university was a very different thing from the stern reproofs, bold invectives, burning remonstrances, prophet-like appeals of William Perkins. What was now cultivated and extolled was a frivolous, florid eloquence, that boasted itself on its deftly-turned tropes, its high-flown paraphrases of the classics, especially Seneca and Cicero, and the Fathers, the multiplied quotations of the 'sermons' published shewing like purple patches on a thread-bare robe. There was trick of manner, mellifluous cadence, simpering refinement, nothing more. The Senhouses *et hoc genus omne* sprinkled *eau-de-cologne* over their hearers (if they durst, it had been '*holy* water'), while parched lips were athirst for the '*living* water'— tickled the ear when the heavily-laden soul sought pardon, the weary rest, the bruised balm. The cross lifted up on Calvary beneath the pallid heavens—the cross as proclaimed by Paul—was 'vulgar,' and to be kept out of sight. The awful blood must first be wiped off—the coarse nails withdrawn. Whoso gainsays, let him turn to their extant 'Sermons.' But amid the faithless some faithful were found. There were some not ashamed of *the* gospel,' some who could stand and withstand 'the loud laugh.' The 'townspeople' would have that which the 'collegians' (so they called them) rejected. In such circumstances we may conceive that the ministry of Sibbes could scarcely fail to be a ministry of power. 'The Day' alone will fully reveal its fruits.

CHAPTER IV.

'PREACHER' AT GRAY'S INN, LONDON.

'Deprived' of Lectureship and 'Outed' from Fellowsnip—Sir Henry Yelverton— 'Preacher' at Gray's Inn—Correction of date—The 'Chapel'—The 'Inn'—Segar MS.—The Auditory—Lord Bacon.

From 1610 to 1615, Sibbes held his lectureship and other honours without molestation. But in the latter year he was deprived ('outed,' says Clarke) both of his fellowship and lecture. Even thus early Laud was at work against all Puritanism and 'preaching ;' and this was the manner of his working. However, as in many other instances, while there was unquestionable hardship and hurt done by the double deprivation, it 'fell out for the furtherance of the gospel.' Sir Henry Yelverton, that 'constant patron to godly ministers,' stepped in and secured the 'preachership' of 'Gray's Inn.' London, for him. All preceding authorities give 1618—the 'Synod of Dort' year—or 'about 1618,' as the date of this well-timed appointment. This is incorrect. I found the following entry in the 'Order-Books:' *

'Quinto die, Feb. A.D. 1616.

'At this penton [pension] Mr Richd. Sibbs is chosen preacher of Graies Inne ; and it is ordered that he shal be continually resident, and shall not take any other benefice or livinge.' †

This appointment introduced him at a bound to the first society of the metropolis.

Among the treasures of the British Museum is a noble folio, drawn up from the books of 'Gray's Inn,' by Segar, one of the society's former 'butlers.' ‡ In it, with superb blazonry of shield and scutcheon, and all the 'pomp of heraldry,' are registered the names of those who were resident 'readers, benchers, ancients, barristers, students,' from the earliest date. If one had the Greek of Homer, or the 'large utterance' of Milton, or even the rhetoric of Macaulay, it were possible to revivify the auditory of the 'chapel.' A more illustrious can scarcely be imagined. The flower of the old nobility, the greatest names of the state and of history, men who mark epochs, were embraced in it. I have looked through the roll from 1616 to 1635—the period of Sibbes's office—and almost at random I note Abbots and Ashleys, Audleys and Amhersts, Bacons and Barnardistons, Boyles and Brookes, Bradshaws and Barrows, Cromwells and Cholmleys, Cornwallises

---

* 'Order Books.' These are deposited at 'Gray's Inn,' where I had the privilege of an unrestricted examination of them. The volume from which I make all my excerpts, is a huge folio, marked 'Gray's Inn. Book of Orders. II. of Eliz. to XVIII. of Chs. II.'

† 'Chapel' of 'Gray's Inn.' I cull from the above authority a record of the foundation of the 'preachership' to which Sibbes was elected :—

CHAPELL.

'It appeareth as well by a deed of the Cort of Augmentacons, bearinge date the 10th of November, in ye 33th (sic) yeare of ye reigne of King Henry 8. As also by an Exemplificacon thereof, made ye 12th November in ye said yeare. As also by another Exemplificacon thereof, granted by ye late Queen Elizab., dated at Westminster the 12th of ffebruary, in the fourth yeare of her reigne. That ye treasurer of ye Cort of Augmentacons, of ye said revenue of ye crowne, for the time beinge, should yearely pay out of ye said treasurres to ye treasurer of ye house of Graye's Inn, Nigh Holborne, in ye county of Midd. for ye time being, ye sume of vi xiij ̄iiij^d (£6, 13s. 4d.), in recompense of a yearly stipend of vij xiij iiij (£7, 13s. 4d.), wch. was duely proved before ye said Cort of Augmentacons to be issuinge out of ye possessions of ye late monasterie of St Bartholomew in Smithfield, besides London ; and of right payable, time out of mind, by ye prior and convent of the said monastrie and their p'decessors, for ye findinge of a chaplaine to celebrate divine service in ye chapell of Graye's Inn aforesaid, for ye students, gent., and fellowes of ye said house,' &c. &c. &c.

‡ 'Segar.' Harleian MSS., 1912. 94, c. 25. Plut. xlvii. E folio.

and Chetwinds, Drakes and Egertons, Fairfaxes and Fitzgeralds, Nevills and Pelhams, Riches and Sidneys, Staffords and Stanleys, Standishes and Talbots, Wallers, and Vaughans, and Veres.* Truly the wheel-wright's son has a worthy audience; ay, and what is better, he is worthy of the audience.

At the date of Sibbes's appointment, the greatest of all the names enumerated, Francis Bacon, had 'chambers' in Gray's Inn; and, after his fall, was a permanent resident.† When it was dark with him, he had Sibbes for his 'preacher.' Am I wrong in thinking that the touching appeal of the stricken Lord Chancellor to his peers, recorded by every biographer, 'I am a *bruised reed,*' may have been a reminiscence of the golden-syllabled words which he had heard from the 'preacher' at Gray's Inn?

I know not that the author of the Bruised Reed is once named

* 'Gray's Inn.' I may give in a foot-note, from Segar's folio, the earlier history of the Society with which the name of Sibbes is so indissolubly associated. Having recited certain ancient mediæval-Latin records, which are also supplemented by prior relations to the Dean and Chapter of St Paul's, the chronicler proceeds:—

'By all wch severall offices, it appeares that the said manor of Portepole, now Gray's Inne, or within ye which a part of Graye's Inne is now situate, was anciently the Inheritance of the Grayes. But I do not find in any of ye said former, &c. . . . that any Gray, lord or owner of ye said manor or messuage, did at any time reside there. Reginald de Gray, in ye 44th year of ye reign of Kinge Edw. 3, for ye yearly rent of Q (?), as is mentioned in ye office, then found after his decease. And in ye wch office (the same beinge in form^r inquisitions named mesuagium), is thereby found to be hospitium and in lease whereby it's manifested yt. ye house then and yet knowne by the name of Gray's Inn, was demised to some p'sons of speciall regard and rank, *and not to meane ones, or p'sons of meane or privat behav^r*, but to such as were united into a Society p'fessinge ye lawes, that in those dayes begunn to congregat and setle themselves within ye Court (?) as an associated company entertayning hospitalitie together. And then this house grew to be off an higher title in denominacon and became to be totally termed by ye Intitulacon of Hospitium in Portopole. And it also appeareth that ye said Reginald de Gray devised ye said messuage as aforesaid in ye reigne of King Edw. 3, in his life-time, and at his death was held for hospitium and by the jury before whom ye said inquisition was taken in ye said 44th yeare of Edw. 3d (a° 1370), was found to bee hospitium, and not mesuaginm. Imediatly whereupon ye said hospitium is called Grey's Inne, or Hospitium Graiorum, for that that estate had been soe long and by soe many severall descents in yt name,' &c. &c. &c.

This quaint and curious narrative, which I believe is now for the first time pub-lished, explains the origin of the name 'Gray's Inn.' Those interested will find much additional information in Segar,—all the more valuable that many of the originals were destroyed by a fire at Gray's Inn. These missing portions have been transcribed, but not very accurately, for the Hon. Society.

† 'Bacon and Gray's Inn.' See an interesting chapter of an unusually interest-ing, but not very accurate, book, Meteyard's 'Hallowed Spots of Ancient London' (4to, 1862), entitled 'York House, Strand, and Gray's Inn,' pp. 80–99. An engrav-ing of 'Gray's Inn' is given on page 90. I need hardly say that all the old build-ings, and the 'faire gardenne,' with its Bacon-planted elms, have long disappeared.

in all Bacon's writings, but then neither is Shakespeare. Still, I cannot help rejoicing that, in his closing years of humiliation and penitence, while he was building up the Cyclopean masonry of his 'Novum Organum,' he had Richard Sibbes to lift his thoughts higher. I delight to picture to myself the mighty thinker and the heavenly preacher walking in the 'faire gardenne' of the Inn, holding high and sanctified discourse.* I fancy I can trace the influence of Sibbes on Bacon, and of Bacon on Sibbes. There are in Sibbes many aphoristic sayings, pregnant seeds of thought, felicitous 'similies' (so marked on the early margins), that bear the very mintage of the 'Essays ;' and again there is in them an insight into Scripture, a working in of its cloth-of-gold with his own meditations, an apposite quotation of its facts and words, that surely came of the sermons and private talk under the elms with Sibbes. It is something to know that two such men knew each other.

The 'Bruised Reed' and 'Soul's Conflict,' and indeed nearly all his works, present specimens of the kind of preaching to which the auditory of 'Gray's Inn' listened from Sunday to Sunday. One is gladdened to think that such men heard such preaching, so wise, so grave, so fervid, so Christful. There grew out of it life-long friendships.

CHAPTER V.

PROVOSTSHIP OF TRINITY COLLEGE, DUBLIN.

Archbishop Ussher—Dr John Preston—Letter of Sibbes—Sir William Temple— Letters of Ussher to Archbishop Abbot and the Hon. Society of Gray's Inn— Sibbes to Ussher—Archbishop Abbot to Ussher—Declines the Provostship.

Installed as 'preacher' at Gray's Inn, Sibbes seems to have acted up to the letter of his appointment; which, it will be remembered, required that he was 'to be continually resident,' and 'to take no other benefice or living.' This he continued apparently to do, with the exception of occasional 'sermons' in the 'city' or in Cambridge, until 1626. In that year new honours came to him. Archbishop Ussher sought to have him made provost of Trinity College, Dublin; and he was elected, on the death of Dr John Hills, 'Master' of St Katherine Hall (now College), Cambridge. A very interesting correspondence remains in relation to

* One asks wistfully if they took any note of one William Shakespeare, who, within three months of the appointment to the 'preachership' at 'Gray's Inn,' was laid beside his little Hamnet by the Avon! (Died, 23d April 1616.)

the former, which I would now introduce. He had long been in intimate friendship with the illustrious primate of Ireland, who, on his visits to London, was wont to invite himself to his 'study.' * One early notice of their mutual regard is contained in a portion of a letter from Dr John Preston to Ussher. It is as follows: 'March 16. 1619.—Your papers you shall surely have with you ; and if there be no remedy that I cannot see you myself, I shall entreat you *to make plain to Mr Sibbes* (or whom else you will) the last point especially, when the LXX weeks began, though I should speak to you about many other things.' † The following brief letter of Sibbes himself a few years onward, 1622, gives us a further glimpse of their relations, as well as of various memorable names and occurrences. Ussher was then Bishop of Meath.

Mr R. Sibbs to the Bishop of Meath.‡

I could not, Right Reverend Sir, omit so fit an opportunity of writing unto you as the coming of two of my worthy friends, Sir Nathaniel Rich and Mr Crew ; though it were but to signify unto you that I retain a thankful and respectful remembrance of your lordship's former love and kindness. Mr Crew is already known unto you ; Sir Nathaniel, I think, a stranger yet unto you ; you shall find him for sincerity, wisdom, and right judgment worthy your inward acquaintance. How matters stand here you shall have better information from those worthy gentlemen than from me. For Cambridge matters, I suppose your lordship hath already heard that Dr Ward is chosen professor in Dr Davenant's place ; there is hope of Mr Preston's coming to be lecturer at Lincoln's Inn, which place is now void. Mrs More, Mr Drake and his wife, Mr Dod, with others that love you heartily in the Lord, are in good health, the Lord be praised. Sir Henry Savil hath ended his days, secretary Murray succeeding him in Eton, but report will prevent my letter in this and other matters. Sir, I long to see your begun historical discourse of the perpetual continuity of a visible church, lengthened and brought to these latter times. No one point will stop the clamour of our adversaries more, nor furnish the weaker with a better plea. Others not very well affected to the Waldenses, &c., for some tenets . . . have gone about to prove what you do some other ways. But perhaps the present exigence of your Church is such as taketh up your daily endeavours and thoughts. And I know the zeal of your heart for the public good will put you forward for whatsoever is for the best advantage of the common cause. I fear lest the encountering with that daring chal-

* 'Ussher and Sibbes.' Brook's 'Lives of the Puritans,' vol. ii. p. 416. From Brook's own copy, interleaved and containing additional MS. notes. In the library of Joshua Wilson, Esq., Tunbridge Wells.

† 'Preston and Ussher.' This and the succeeding correspondence I take from 'The whole Works of the Most Rev. James Ussher, D.D., Lord Archbishop of Armagh and Primate of all Ireland. With a Life of the Author, and an Account of his Writings. By Charles Richard Elrington, D.D., Regius Professor of Divinity in the University of Dublin. Dublin: Hodges & Smith. 16 vols. 8vo, 1847, *seq.*' See vol. xvi. p. 873. Elrington supersedes Parr (who also gives the most of the letters), and I therefore take the whole from him.

‡ 'Sibbes to Usher.' Letter ccclxiii. Vol. xvi. p. 395, 396.

lenger breed you a succession of troubles. How far you have proceeded in this matter we know not. The Lord lead you through all conflicts and businesses, with comfortable evidence of his wisdom in guiding you, and goodness in a blessed issue.

Your Lordship's in all Christian affection and service,

R. SIBBES.

Gray's Inn, March 21. 1622.

Advancing to 1626–27, Ussher was now archbishop and primate, and involved in an imbroglio of political and ecclesiastical difficulties. His was only a splendid exile. He writes, half-mournfully half in dread, under date ' Feby. 9th, 1626 :'—' As for the general state of things here, they are so desperate that I am afraid to write anything thereof.'* He was specially ' troubled' in the matter of ' Trinity College,' of which he was the patron. Sir William Temple was provost, and from his great age, utterly inefficient, and even in dotage. There were perpetual disputes between him and the ' fellows,' so much so that the removal of the provost, in some quiet manner, was felt to be the only method of preserving the discipline and good order of the college. To this Ussher addressed himself, and ultimately persuaded the old man—a not unhistoric name—to resign, on condition that Sibbes took his place. This we learn from a letter of the primate to Archbishop Abbot, to whom, on 10th January 1626–27, he writes :—' The time is now come wherein we have at last wrought upon Sir William Temple to give up his place, *if the other may be drawn over.*' That ' other' was Sibbes. But all difficulty about the resignation, with or without conditions, was unexpectedly removed by the death of Sir William, who expired on the 15th of January 1626–27, five days only after the date of Ussher's letter,—upon which he again wrote Abbot in favour of Sibbes. The whole correspondence is of the last interest, and is self-explanatory. It may now be given in order, the more so, that, excepting one of the letters, it has been overlooked or left unused :—

The Archbishop of Armagh to the most Reverend GEORGE ABBOT, *Archbishop of Canterbury.*†

MY MOST GRACIOUS LORD,—When I took my last leave of you at Lambeth, I made bold to move your grace for the settlement of the provostship of our college here upon some worthy man, whensoever the place should become void. I then recommended unto you Mr Sibbes, the preacher of Gray's Inn, with whose learning, soundness of judgment, and uprightness of life I was very well acquainted ; and it pleased your grace to listen unto my motion, and give way to the coming over of the person named, when time required. The time, my lord, is now come, wherein we have at last wrought Sir William Temple to give up his place, if the other may be

* Ussher, xv. 365–6.   † Ussher, letter cxxi. xv. 361–2.

drawn over. And therefore I most humbly entreat your grace to give unto Mr Sibbes that encouragement he deserveth ; in whose behalf I dare undertake that he shall be as observant of you, and as careful to put in execution all your directions, as any man whosoever. The matter is of so great importance for the good of this poor church, and your fatherly care, as well of the church in general, as our college in particular, so well known, that I shall not need to press you herein with many words. And therefore, leaving it wholly to your grace's grave consideration, and beseeching Almighty God to bless you in the managing of your weighty employments, I humbly take my leave, and rest,

Your grace's in all duty, ready to be commanded,

J. A.

Drogheda, January 10. 1626.

At the same time, the primate addressed a similar letter to the 'Honourable Society of Gray's Inn,' to deprecate their putting any obstacles in the way of Sibbes's acceptance. By a slip of the pen, he inserts—'*Lincoln's*,' instead of 'Gray's' Inn. As himself formerly 'preacher' in 'Lincoln's,' the mistake was natural :—

*The Archbishop of Armagh to the Honourable Society of Gray's-Inn.**

MY MOST WORTHY FRIENDS,—I cannot sufficiently express my thankfulness unto you for the honour which you have done unto me, in vouchsafing to admit me into your society, and to make me a member of your own body. Yet so is it fallen out for the present, that I am enforced to discharge one piece of debt with entering into another. For thus doth the case stand with us. Sir William Temple, who hath governed our college at Dublin these seventeen years, finding age and weakness now to increase upon him, hath resolved to ease himself of that burthen, and resign the same to some other. Now of all others whom we could think of, your worthy preacher Mr Sibbes is the man upon whom all our voices have here settled, as one that hath been well acquainted with an academical life, and singularly well qualified for the undertaking of such a place of government. I am not ignorant what damage you are to sustain by the loss of such an able man, with whose ministry you have been so long acquainted ; but I consider withal, that you are at the well-head, where the defect may quickly be supplied ; and that it somewhat also tendeth to the honour of your Society, that out of all the king's dominions your house should be singled out for the place unto which the seminary of the whole Church in this kingdom should have recourse for help and succour in this case. And therefore my most earnest suit unto you is, that you would give leave unto Mr Sibbes to repair hither, at leastwise for a time, that he may see how the place will like him. For which great favour our whole Church shall be obliged unto you : and I, for my part, shall evermore profess myself to rest

Your own in all Christian service, Ready to be commanded,

J. A.

Drogheda, January 10. 1626.

Further :—

The Archbishop of Armagh to the most Reverend GEORGE ABBOT, *Archbishop of Canterbury.*†

MY VERY GOOD LORD,—I wrote unto your grace heretofore concerning

* Ussher, letter cxx., xv. 363-4. † Ussher, letter cxxi., xv. 365.

the substitution of Mr Sibbes into the place of Sir William Temple. But having since considered with myself how some occasions may fall out that may hinder him from coming hither, and how many most unfit persons are now putting in for that place, I have further emboldened myself to signify thus much more of my mind unto you, that in case Mr Sibbes do not come unto us, I cannot think of a more worthy man, and more fitted for the government of that college, than Mr Bedel, who hath heretofore remained with Sir Henry Wotton at Venice, and is now beneficed about Berry. If either he, or Dr Featly, or any other worthy man whom you shall think fit, can be induced to accept of the place; and your grace will be pleased to advise the fellows of the college to elect him thereunto ; that poor house shall ever have cause to bless your memory for the settlement of it at such a time as this, where so many labour to make a prey of it.

Of the ' occurrences' that might ' fall out' to hinder Sibbes from coming, the primate had been informed in our next letter :—

MR R. SIBBES *to the Archbishop of Armagh.**

RIGHT REV. AND MY VERY GOOD LORD,—I answered your letters presently upon the receipt of them, but out of a mind diversely affected as divers things presented themselves to me ; it much moved me when I perceived your great care of the place, the cost, the trouble, the more than ordinary inclination towards me, far beyond any deserts of mine. Yet as I signified to your grace, when I consider God's providence in raising me so little before, to another place, and that compatible with my present employment here in London, it moveth me to think it were rash to adventure upon another place. And I have entered into a course of procuring some good to the college, which is like to be frustrate, if I now leave them, and they exposed to some who intend to serve their own turn of them. The scandal whereof would lie upon me. The judgment of my friends here is for my stay, considering I am fixed already, and there must be a call for a place ; as to a place, they allege the good which may be done, and doubtfulness of good succession here ; and that it were better that some other man had that place that were not so fixed here. These and such like considerations move them to think, that when your lordship shall know how it is with me at this time, that you will think of some other successor. Nothing of a great time so much troubled me. I humbly desire you, my lord, to take in good part this my not accepting, considering now there be other difficulties than were when you were in England with us. It is not yet openly known that I refuse it, that so you may have time of pitching upon another. I write now this second time, fearing lest my former letter might miscarry. I could set the comfort by you against many objections, were not that late chief in Cambridge. I count it one part of my happiness in especial manner, that ever I knew your lordship ; the remembrance of you will be fresh in my heart whilst I live, which will move me to desire the multiplying of all happiness upon you and yours.

I have not delivered the letter to my lord of Canterbury, because it hath reference to the business as it concerneth me. The Lord continue to honour you in his service for the good of many, and to keep you in these dangerous times.—Your Grace's to command in the Lord,

R. SIBBES.

Gray's Inn, Feb. 7. A.D. 1626.

I humbly desire you to remember my service and respects to Mrs Ussher.

* Ussher, letter ccclxxxvi., x vi. 440-1.

Upon receipt of this the primate wrote :*—' But now very lately, even by the last packet, I have received a letter from Mr Sibbs, signifying his doubtfulness of accepting the place of provost here (he having beïne *at the same time* chosen head of another college in Cambridge), which hath much altered our intentions.' A few days later, Ussher was informed more definitely by Dr Samuel Ward of Sibbes's election to the Mastership of ' Catherine Hall.' I give an extract, with context, as it introduces to us an eminent ornament of Sibbes's circle :—

Dr SAMUEL WARD *to* USSHER—London, ' Feb. 13. 1626.'†

The 25th of January deceased your good friend and mine, Mr Henry Alvey, at Cambridge. I was with him twice when he was sick : the first time I found him sick, but very patient and comfortable. He earnestly prayed that God would give him patience and perseverance. The later time I came he was in a ' slumber, and did speak nothing : I prayed for him, and then departed. Shortly after he departed this life. He desired to be buried privately, and in the churchyard, and in a sheet only, without a coffin, for so, said he, was our Saviour. But it was thought fitting he should be put in a coffin, and so he was : I was at his interring the next day at night. Thus God is daily collecting his saints to himself. The Lord prepare us all for the *dies ascensionis*, as St Cyprian styleth it. Since the death of Dr Walsall, Dr Goslin, our vice-chancellor, and Dr Hill, master of St Katherine Hall, are both dead. In their places succeed, in Bennet College, Dr Butts ; in Caius College, Mr Bachcroft, one of the fellows ; *in Katherine Hall, Mr Sibbes of Gray's Inn.*

Notwithstanding Sibbes's intimation, that he had not delivered the primate's letter to Abbot, he must have subsequently changed his mind, and done so. To Ussher's recommendation, Archbishop Abbot lent a cordially willing ear. This appears by his letter in reply, which would also seem to indicate that Sibbes had been persuaded to go over to Ireland, probably to consult personally with his friend :—

The most Reverend GEORGE ABBOT, *Archbishop of Canterbury, to the Archbishop of Armagh.*‡

MY VERY GOOD LORD,—I send unto you Mr Sibbes, who can best report what I have said unto him. I hope that college shall in him have a very good master, which hitherto it hath not had. You shall make my excuse to the fellows that I write not unto them. You shall do well to pray to God that he will bless his church; but be not too solicitous in that matter, which will fall of itself, God Almighty being able and ready to support his own cause. But of all things take heed that you project no new ways; for if they fail you shall bear a grievous burden; if they prosper, there shall be no thanks to you. Be patient, and tarry the Lord's leisure. And so commending me unto you, and to the rest of your brethren, I leave you to the Almighty, and remain,

Your lordship's loving brother,   G. CANT.

Lambeth, March 19. 1626.

Sibbes no doubt found, on his arrival in Dublin, that the ' place

* Ussher, letter cccxci., xvi. 453.   † Ussher, xv. 369.   ‡ Ussher, xv. 375

33

was likely to prove harassing, and to lead him into controversy. A sentence from a letter of Joseph Mede, in like circumstances, explains his declinature :—' I would not,' he writes to Ussher, ' be willing to adventure into a strange country upon a litigious title, having seen the bad experience at home of perpetual jars and discontents from such beginnings.' * Similar reasons, combined with the attractions of Gray's Inn and Cambridge, led Sibbes to return, leaving the provostship of Trinity College, Dublin, to be filled by the afterwards revered Bishop Bedell.

CHAPTER VI.

MASTER OF CATHARINE HALL, CAMBRIDGE.

Accepts Mastership—Relaxation of ' order' at Gray's Inn—Founder of Catharine Hall and its celebrities—Its condition—' Troublous times'—Dr John Preston—Trinity Lectureship—Bishopric declined—Friendship between Sibbes and Preston—Fellow-labourers—Conversion of Preston—The effect of the preaching of the two Puritan Masters—Auditory of St Mary's—Memorials of Trinity Lecture—Success of Sibbes as Master—Clarke and Fuller—Fellows.

Having declined the Provostship of Trinity College, Dublin, Sibbes at once accepted the Mastership of Catharine Hall, Cambridge, to which, as has been narrated, he was almost simultaneously elected. No record remains of the influence used to secure this coveted and often contested honour for the ' outed' Fellow and ' deprived' Lecturer. It is not improbable that it was to Dr John Preston, the Puritan Master of the 'nest of Puritans' (so his enemies designated it), Emmanuel, that he was indebted. Preston was then in the height of his favour with the Duke of Buckingham,—the acceptance of whose patronage is one of the stains upon the memory of the Puritans. He had long been in close friendship with the preacher of Gray's Inn.

There must have been some relaxation of the ' order' under which Sibbes accepted the appointment of preacher to Gray's Inn,—to admit of his accepting the mastership of Catharine Hall, without resignation of the other. The statute is very explicit, as will be seen :—' 15 Nov. 40 Eliz. (1598-9).—The divinity-reader to be chosen shall be nominated, having *no ecclesiastical preferment* other than a prebend without cure of souls, nor readership in any other place ; and shall keep the same place as long as he continues thus qualified, and no longer ; and to be charged with reading but twice a week, except when there is a communion.'†

* Ussher, as *ante*, p. 455-56, vol. xvi.

† This ' order' was made in the term previous to the election of the successor of

There were then, as now, the two distinct offices of reader, some-times called chaplain, and of preacher, sometimes called lecturer, and as in above order, 'divinity-reader.'* So that it was the more easy to arrange for Sibbes's absence during the week. From an entry, under date 19th Jan. 1612, we learn that ' The preacher, ye chap-lain, ye steward . . . . . . were to be allowed such commons as *gentlemen.*'† Not as 'gentleman' merely, but as associate and friend, was Sibbes regarded. The anxiety of the ' ancients, barris-ters, students,' to retain his services, would also smoothe the way to place in practical desuetude the ' order' as to '*no other ecclesiastical preferment.*' Be all this as it may, Sibbes entered on the master-ship of Catharine Hall forthwith. ‡

Catharine or Katharine Hall, on whose Mastership Sibbes thus entered, was then, as it continues, one of the minor Colleges of the University. Yet is it not without its own celebrities, even the foremost names of English theology, Church and Puritan, before and since. It proudly tells of John Bradford the martyr, John Maplet, John Overall, William Strong, Ralph Robinson, Ralph Brownrig, John Arrowsmith, William Spurstowe, James Shirley (the dramatist), John Lightfoot, Thomas Goodwin, John Ray, Wil-liam Wotton, John Strype, Thomas Sherlock, Joseph Milner, and has recently lost Charles Hardwick. It was founded by a Robert Woodlark, D.D.,§ (whose name has passed away like his namesake's song of a previous summer), in 1475 ; and took its name in honour of the ' virgin and martyr St Katherine.' Its original endowment, beyond ' the tenements and garden,' was small for even those days.

a certain Dr Crooke, who was preacher from 1583 to 1599. His successor was a Mr Fenton, elected 7th Feb., 41st Eliz., 1598–99. In respect to the preacher being unmarried, the ' order' was rigid, and probably explains why Sibbes remained so to the end. I cull a couple of entries that don't say very much for the chivalry of the Gray's Inn authorities :—1612, 'A ffine paid upon change of life.' 1630, ' Noe women to come into any pt. of ye Chapell.' 1647, 'No familie to bee in the house.'—Segar MS.

* ' Chaplain.'—I note certain little memoranda in relation to the ' Chaplain,' as distingushed from the ' preacher :' the later from Segar, being one of the items included in the destroyed originals—the warrrant itself having perished ; and the earlier from the ' order book' at Gray's Inn :—1625, Warrant (granted) to pay to the treasurer of Gray's Inn £6 : 13 : 4, June 25. yearly, during pleasure, for a chap-lain to read service daily in the chapel there. An earlier entry runs thus :—' 5th Feb. 1620. Mr Finch allowed 4/ a week for reading in the Chappell.'

† ' Order-Book' Gray's Inn, p. 16, Segar MS.

‡ In Carter's History of the University of Cambridge (pp. 202–6), and Graduati Cantabrigienses, Dr Brownrig is erroneously stated to have been elected Master of Catharine Hall in 1631. Even so accurate a writer as Mr Russell (' Memorials of Fuller', p. 114) repeats the blunder.

§ ' Dr Woodelark.' The Cambridge Antiquarian Society have published a Cata-logue of Books presented by the founder to ' Catharine Hall.'

It had some subsequent 'benefactors,' among whom appear, earlier and later, Barnardistons and Claypoles. At the period of Sibbes's election, the buildings were dilapidated, the revenues limited, the students few in number. But he threw his whole soul into his office, and speedily not only attracted a fair share of young men, but also persuaded his many noble and wealthy friends to become 'benefactors.' So early as 1630, there were no fewer than twenty-eight new entries of students ; and, by that time, the hall was renovated and adorned.

Sibbes entered on his mastership in 'troublous times.' When deprived of his 'lectureship' at Trinity—which in all probability, as we said, originated with the memorial addressed to him by the parishioners—he was succeeded by a John Jeffrey, of Pembroke Hall, who resigned in 1624. Upon his resignation a remarkable contest for the situation ensued. The 'townsmen'—who were now leavened with Puritanism through his preaching, and that of his associates—were desirous of electing Dr Preston ; and to make it better worth his acceptance, raised the stipend from £40 or £50, to £80 a year. He was opposed by Paul Micklethwaite, fellow of Sidney College, who was supported by the Bishop of Ely, Francis White, a creature of Laud's, and the heads of colleges. It is difficult to understand on what plea there was interference with the 'townsmen.' They had themselves originated the lectureship ; had themselves appointed Sibbes, had themselves supported it. But the matter came before the king at Royston, and so intense was the royal wish to root out Puritanism, his primate inciting him to the dastardly work, that Dr Preston was actually offered a bishopric, the see of Gloucester being then void. He refused to withdraw. He accepted and entered upon the lectureship. All honour to the man who spurned a mitre, its honours and revenues alike, when offered at the price of proving false to the earnest desires of 'the people' to have the gospel, the very gospel, preached to them,—wherein, in the high but truthful encomium of Goodwin, he did 'bow his more sublime and raised parts to lowest apprehension.'* When Sibbes returned to Cambridge therefore, he found in Preston one like-minded, while equally did Preston find in him one worthy to stand by his side, and 'display a banner because of the truth.'

Preston and Sibbes, from the date of the mastership of the latter, were the two great centres of influence in Cambridge, in so far as the *preaching* of the gospel was concerned. They loved one another with a love that was something wonderful. They were as

* To the Reader. . . . Sermons before His Majesty, 1630. 4to.

David and Jonathan in earlier, and as Luther and Melanchthon in later, days. They were never found apart when anything was to be done for THEIR MASTER. To the last it was so ; and when the prematurely old Master of 'Emmanuel' died, he left all his papers to his beloved friend the Master of Catharine Hall, along with John Davenport, sending words of kindly greeting by Lord Say and Seale to Gray's Inn. As Sibbes's return to Cambridge, and association with Preston, formed a marked era in his life and life-work, it is needful to dwell for a little on the history of his friend.

Dr Preston was a man of extraordinary force of character and splendour of eloquence, and burned with the zeal of a seraph. Very remarkable were his antecedents. For years, like John Cotton, he had been the glory of the 'wits' for his learning and faculty of utterance. But by John Cotton's first sermon after his 'change,' he had been smitten as between joints and marrow, soul and spirit, and thenceforward had known nothing but Christ Jesus crucified. Cotton Mather tells the story of his conversion finely, and we may pause over it for a moment. 'Some time after this change upon the soul of Mr Cotton,' he says, 'it came to his turn again to preach at St Mary's ; and because he was to preach, an high expectation was raised through the whole university that they should hear a sermon flourishing indeed with all the learning of the whole university. Many difficulties had Mr Cotton in his own mind, and what course to steer.' And then he proceeds to tell how he decided ' to preach a plain sermon, even such a sermon as in his own conscience he thought would be most pleasing unto the Lord Jesus Christ ; and he discoursed practically and powerfully, but very solidly, upon the plain doctrine of repentance.' What then ? 'The vain wits of the university, disappointed thus with a more excellent sermon, that shot some troublesome admonitions into their consciences, discovered their vexation at this disappointment by their not humming, as according to their sinful and absurd custom they had formerly done ; and the vice-chancellor, for the very same reason also, graced him not as he did others that pleased him. Nevertheless,' adds Mather, 'the satisfaction which he enjoyed in his own faithful soul abundantly compensated unto him the loss of any human favour or honour ; nor did he go without many encouragements from some doctors, then having a better sense of religion upon them, who prayed him to persevere in the good way of preaching which he had now taken.' And then he continues, with exultation, 'But perhaps the greatest consolation of all, was a notable effect of the sermon then preached. The famous Dr

MEMOIR OF RICHARD SIBBES, D.D.

Preston, then a fellow of Queen's College in Cambridge, and of great note in the university, came to hear Mr Cotton, with the same "itching ears" as others were then led withal. For some good while after the beginning of the sermon, his frustrated expectation caused him to manifest his uneasiness all the ways that were then possible; but before the sermon was ended, like one of Peter's hearers, he found himself "pierced at the heart." His heart within him was now struck with such resentment of his own interior state before the God of heaven, that he could have no peace in his soul, till, with a "wounded soul," he had repaired unto Mr Cotton, from whom he received those further assistances wherein he became a "spiritual father" unto one of the greatest men in his age.'*

These were men who believed in a 'living,' presiding God, and who were not ashamed to recognise, nor afraid to avouch, 'the finger of God,' the very interference of God, as real as when the Lord met Saul of Tarsus, in the turning of a human soul to Himself. They saw in Sibbes reaching the conscience of John Cotton, and in John Cotton touching the heart of Dr Preston, so many links of the mighty chain of predestination, whose last link is fast to the throne of the Eternal. They are weaker and not wiser men who scorn such faith. It is not to be wondered at, then, that in the correspondence of the Puritans in Cambridge of this period, it was felt to be 'of God,' that quick as one preacher of the word, in its blessed height and depth, breadth and length, was removed thence, another succeeded. William Perkins was taken away, but Paul Bayne was 'sent' in his room. Paul Bayne was removed, and Sibbes was sent; Sibbes was 'outed,' and John Preston took his place; and now while the Master of Emmanuel was longing for one who might be a fellow-helper with him, again came Richard Sibbes. The hearts of the praying few were cheered, and under the awakening, rich, full, grand, proclamations of the 'grace of God that bringeth salvation,' all Cambridge was moved. Preston was from day to day at Emmanuel and Trinity, and Sibbes from day to day at Catharine Hall, preaching as 'dying men to dying men;' knowing nothing among them save Jesus Christ and him crucified, yea, regarding the demand of the 'wits' for 'polite' preaching as but an awful echo of the olden cry, 'Let him come down from the cross and we will believe him.'

From the title-pages of the early editions of their Sermons, we find that they were, again and again, appointed to preach at St Mary's, the church of the whole University. On these occasions

* Magnalia, as *ante* page 16.

38

there was such a galaxy of men assembled as could not have been seen elsewhere in all the world. The effect was electric, among gentle as among simple. It rejoices one to scan the roll of the names of those who were then Masters, Fellows, and Students, and all of whom were found in attendance on the preaching of Sibbes and Preston. With relation to Sibbes, we read 'The Saint's Safety' and 'Christ is Best,' 'Christ's Sufferings for Man's Sin' and 'The Church's Visitation,' and 'The Saints' Hiding-place,' with deepened interest, as, turning to the original title-pages, we find they were addressed to auditories that included the foremost names of the age. The dates inform us that these sermons, which are almost unrivalled for largeness, I might even say grandeur, of thought, richness of gospel statement, impressiveness and pungency of application, and music of diction, were delivered when the several colleges sent to St Mary's names such as these. Foremost stands John Milton, then at Christ's, and himself writing sonnets on the very themes of Sibbes's discourses. Next comes Jeremy Taylor, just entered '*pauper scholaris*,' as Sibbes assumed the Mastership. Behind him, already renowned as a 'public orator,' mark George Herbert. Side by side with him rises the girlish face, with its strange shadow of sorrow, of Matthew Wren, destined to belie God's handwriting in that face, by becoming a 'persecutor.' Very different is the next that meets our eye, William Gouge, of King's. And beside him is one who will be the preacher's successor at Catharine Hall, Ralph Brownrig, looking wistfully upward with his large, beaming eyes. Snug in some sequestered pew, taking keen note of all in that marvellous memory of his, see Thomas Fuller. Worn and weary, yet moved to listen, picture Edmund Castell and Abraham Whelock. Sitting at the foot of the pulpit stairs are Charles Chauncy and Richard Holdsworth, and dreamy Peter Sterry from Emmanuel. Taking notes, and wishing the hour-glass were turned again, is Joseph Mede. Fronting the preacher, and intent as any, lo! the young Lord Wriothesly, son of Shakespeare's Earl of Southampton, and young Sir Dudley North, son of Lord North of Kirkling, both of Sibbes's own college, St John's. Linking himself arm-in-arm with the preacher as he descends, mark stormy John Williams, afterwards Bishop and 'Lord Keeper.' And thus might be recounted, almost by the hundred, names that still shine like a winter's night of stars. St Mary's pews and lobbies, crowded, above and below, with such hearers, to such preachers, is a noticeable mark of progress.*

Perhaps I cannot better illustrate the advance of Puritanism

---

* I have gathered these names, after Masson (Life of Milton, i. 92–99), from numerous sources, but mainly from Cooper's 'Annals of Cambridge,' Wood's 'Athenæ'

in Cambridge than by here submitting a hitherto unpublished document of this period, 1626–27, recovered from the 'Church-wardens' books of the parish.* It very strikingly reveals the interest pervading the community in the Trinity lectureship. The document explains itself. I adhere to its orthography—

'Whereas, such p'sons as are interessed in the seates of the gallerie of this church ("Trinity") to sit there dureinge the time of the lecture, have-inge paid for the same to the p'ish, and yet, notwithstanding, are displaced by others haveinge not interest there, to their greivance and wronge; and, unles redresse herein be speedely had, such p'sons soe greived will with-draw their cotribucons from the said lecture. For remedie whereof, it is ordered and agreed unto, by a joynt consent of all the p'shioners, that from henceforth noe p'son nor p'sons of what condyc'on soever, except such who have interest in the seats, shal be permytted to goe up into the gal-leries untyl the bell have done tollinge; and then, yf any place be voyd, or may be spared to p'mytt, in the first place, grave divines, and after them such others as shall be lyked of by such as shall keep the dore : and yf any who have interest in the seates shall bringe any stranger to be placed there, and will have him to have his place in the gallerie, then such p'son bringing such stranger, to keepe belowe, and take his place els where for such tyme ; and yf any person interessed in the seats doe not repair to the church before the bell have done tollinge, then he to lose his place for that tyme.

'It is likewise ordered, by ye like consent, that such p'sons as have inte-rest in any of ye seates in ye church, shall not have it particularly to them-selves to place and displace whom they will, but only to have ye use of the seats, duringe the tyme of the lecture, for theire owne p'sons, and to receave into them such other of the parish, yf any such come, as shall belonge to such seate, and such others likewise as are people of qualitye who doe con-tribute to ye lecture ; and not to receave any children into their seats.

'It is further ordered that noe seats eyther in ye galleries or in ye church shall hereafter be disposed of to any wth out the consent of the parishiners at a publiq meetinge in the church.†

Thus moving the ' whole city,' Sibbes and Preston went hand-in-hand ; and long after they were gone, when a very different spirit

(by Bliss), Fuller's ' Worthies' (by Nichols), and the ' Lives of Nicholas Ferrar, and of Matthew Robinson,' two of, I trust, a series of like ' Biographies,' under the scho-larly editorial care of Mr Mayor of St John's. Consult also the 'Memoirs' of each name given. All, however, wishing to get real insight into Cambridge-life of the period, I must again and again refer to Mr Masson's 'Milton.' Sibbes's popularity and success is testified by all who write about him, and I can trace none who was so frequently called to preach in St Mary's.

* From ' Between the Churchwarden's Accounts for 1626 and 1627, Trinity Parish, Cambridge.' Kindly pointed out to me by Mr Wallis, and obligingly transcribed, with his usual exactness, by Mr Cooper.

† It may be as well to round off, in a foot-note, such additional memoranda as are in my possession about the lectureship. On 11th May 1630, there was again in-terference and controversy, Dr Thomas Goodwin being the lecturer. A letter respecting it was addressed to the vice-chancellor by Dudley Carleton, Viscount Dor-chester, one of the principal secretaries of state. This ' letter' may be here given from

reigned in Cambridge, born of the wild licence of the Restoration, white-headed men would recall their honoured names with a sigh.

But, while thus faithful as a 'servant of Jesus Christ' in preaching, Richard Sibbes had the faculty of government. Catharine Hall soon found itself on an equality with its sister colleges. He returned from Sunday to Sunday, while the 'Courts' sat, to Gray's Inn, and was ever forward to plead the claims of his 'little house,' with his noble friends there.

We have many testimonies to his influence and usefulness in both. Of the former, Samuel Clarke observes : 'About the year 1618 (1616), he was chosen Preacher to Gray's Inn, one of the learnedest societies in England, where his ministry found such general approbation and acceptance that, besides the learned lawyers of the house, many noble personages, and many of the gentry and citizens, resorted to hear him, and many, till this day

the Baker MSS. (xxvii. 137), as inserted in Cooper's Annals of Cambridge (iii. 229–30).

To my Reverend Friend Mr Dr BUTS, *Vice-chan, &c.*

SIR,—By reason of his Majesties late directions concerning lecturers, that they should read divine service according to the Liturgy, before their lectures, and the afternoone sermons to be turned into catechising, some doubt hath beene made of the continuance of the lecture at Trinity Church, in Cambr. which for many yeares past hath beene held at one of the clocke in the afternoone, without divine service read before yt, and cannot be continued at that hower, if the whole service should be reade before the sermon begin. Whereupon his Majestie hath been informed that the same is a publick lecture, serving for all the parishes in that town (being fourteen in number), and that the university sermon is held at the same tyme, which would be troubled with a greater resort than can be well permitted, yf the towne sermon should be discontinued : and that the same being held at the accustomed hower, there will be tyme enough left after that sermon ended, and the auditory departed thence to their own parish churches, as well for divine service as for catechising in that and all other churches in the towne, which could not well be, yf divine service should be read in that church before the lecture ; besides the catechising in that church, would hereby be lost. Upon these motives his Majesty, being graciously pleased that the said lecture may be continued at the accustomed hower, and in manner as yt hath been heretofore used, hath given me in charge to make knowne to you his royall pleasure accordingly, but under this caution, that not only divine service, but catechising be duely read and used after that sermon ended, both in that and the rest of the churches of the towne ; and that the sermon doe end in convenient tyme for that purpose, soe as no pretext be made, either for the present or in future tyme, by color of the foresaid sermon, to hinder either divine service or catechising, which his Majestie is resolved to have maintained. And so I bidd you heartily farewell, and rest, Yours to doe you service,   DORCHESTER.

From Whitehall, the 11th of May 1630.

Mr Cooper annotates : 'Randolph in a poem "On Importunate Dunnes," after a curious malediction on the Cambridge tradesmen, adds—

" And if this vex 'um not, I'le grive the town,
  With this curse, State, put *Trinity-lecture* down." '

Randolph's Poems, ed. 1648, p. 119.

(1674–77), bless God for the benefit which they received of him.'[*]
Besides this, various regulations and 'orders' as to seats and right
of entrance in the order-books, inform us of over-crowded attendance.
Thus, under 1623, 'All strangers to be kept out of the Chapell at
Sermon, but such as are brought in by some of y[e] society.' Perhaps even more significant of a crowd is what follows : 'And all y[e]
gentlemen to goe out of y[e] Chappell bare-headed in decent manner.'

Of the latter, again, Clarke says, 'About the year 1625, or '26, he
was chosen Master of Katharine Hall in Cambridge, the government
whereof he continued till his dying day ; and, indeed, like a faithful
governor, he was always very solicitous and careful to procure and
advance the good of that little house. For he procured good means
and maintenance, by his interest in many worthy persons, for the
enlargement of the College, and was a means and instrument to
establish learned and religious Fellows there ; inasmuch as, in his
time, it proved a very famous society for piety and learning, both in
Fellows and Scholars.'[†] To the same effect, though with characteristic quaintness, Fuller testifies, 'He found the House in a mean
condition, the wheel of St. Katharine having stood still (not to say
gone backwards) for some years together ; he left it replenished with
scholars, beautified with buildings, better endowed with revenues.'[‡]
Somewhat boastfully, perhaps, Daniel Milles, in his list of Masters,
thus describes Sibbes :—

'Ricardus Sibbs, Sacræ Theologiæ Professor,[§] omnium quos præsens
ætas viderit vir pientissimus, concionator mellitissimus, qui haud paucorum
corda suavitate dicendi emolliit, et vivendi sanctitate ad bonam frugem
plane rapuit. Hic erat qui collegium istud partim temporum injuria,
partim Præfectorum socordia et avaritia bonis suis spoliatum, et omni
honore exutum, ad pristinam famam et dignitatem restituit, quiaque erat
apud omnes pios autoritate maximâ, largam benefactorum messem, in hoc
vacuum gymnasium feliciter diduxit. Adeo ut non nudo Præfecti nomine
dignus videatur, sed alter fundator censeri debeat.'

Other testimonies, as of Eachard,[||] might be given, were it needful ;
and, indeed, the tribute of Sir Philip Sidney to Hubert Languet
must have been his, from many,

> ". . . . . hating what is naught,
> For faithful heart, clean hands, and mouth as true.
> With his sweet skill my skill-less youth he drew
> To have a feeling taste of Him that sits
> Beyond the heaven, *far more beyond our wits.*'
> (*Arcadia*, Book iii. pp. 397–8, ed. 1755.)

Of the Fellows, during Sibbes's Mastership, may be named Anthony

* 'Clarke,' as *ante*, p. 144.　　　† 'Clarke,' as *ante*, p. 144.
‡ Fuller, 'Worthies,' edited by Nichols. 2 vols. 4to. 1811. Vol. ii. p. 343.
§ *i.e.*, D.D.　　　|| 'Eachard,' History of England, p. 451.

Pym (1628), probably a relative of *the* John Pym, who was a personal friend, and mentioned in his will; William Spurstowe (1630);* John Sibbes (1631), his nephew; Charles Pym (1631), brother of Anthony; Roger Fleetwood (1632); Joseph Spurstowe (1634).

CHAPTER VII.

SIBBES AND LAUD—' THE PALATINATE.'

The Puritans watched—The Elector Palatine—Disasters—Shame of England—
Battle of Prague—Frederick and Elizabeth fugitives—Persecution—Circular
Letter by Sibbes, Gouge, Taylor, and Davenport—Citation before the Star-
Chamber—Pronounced ' Notorious Delinquents.'

All the emotion and interest to hear such preaching as was that of Sibbes and Preston, while it gives a measure of the progress of Puritanism (using the word in its recognised historic and lustrous sense), is also to the student of the period a measure of the hate with which the king (in so far as he had stamina enough to hate) and Bishop Laud, now rising into notice, regarded it. So early as 1611, the latter was a '*whisperer,*' a '*busy-body,*' ever going about with sly, stealthy-paced, panther-like foot-fall, and keen, cold eye, if by any means, he might possess himself of *secrets.* · Between Gray's inn, and Catharine Hall, and St Mary's, with not unfrequent ' sermons' elsewhere, Sibbes had noble vantage-ground for noble service, and he was occupying it to the full; and Laud was ready to pounce upon him. I have now to narrate the occasion. Sibbes was not a man to narrow his activities to his own immediate sphere, or to his own country. He watched with profoundest interest the progress of the great Protestant sister-countries, rejoicing in their joy and mourning with their mourning. In 1620, he had spoken burning words ' of the Palatinate ;' words that reveal the common shame of England for her king's pusillanimous desertion of the Elector Frederick, a man true and good in himself, and knit by the tenderest ties to the king of England. From shore to shore the nation had rung with acclaim over revolting Bohemia—the land of John Huss and many martyr-names. They had said ' Amen' to the rejection of Ferdinand II., and their hearts beat high for the Elector Palatine chosen in his stead, when he fearlessly said ' Yes' to the call. History tells the tragic sequel.

* Spurstowe. The date, 1630, of Spurstowe's ' fellowship' (he was afterwards Master), shews that Mr Masson has made a slip in enumerating his name among the distinguished ' fellows' under Dr Hill's Mastership. Life of Milton, i. 97. I cannot make even this small reference to Mr Masson without, in common with every literary man since the issue of his book, acknowledging my indebtedness to his industry, and almost prodigal elucidation and illustration of contemporary events and names.

Then opened what proved the 'Thirty Years' War,' in which the emperor, and pope, and the king of Spain were leagued against Frederick, and against the Protestant Union in him. All Europe looked on. Our own England was humiliated, all but treasonous, as James talked his foolish talk and lived his unclean life, and forgot daughter, son-in-law, Protestantism—all. Driven to do something, he did his little when too late. In November 1620, the Protestants were smitten in one decisive battle—Prague ; and Frederick and his queen, losing Bohemia, losing the Palatinate, losing all, fled as refugees to Holland. What followed, only the great sealed 'book' above will declare. The triumphant enemy 'played havoc ;' and, through many dark and terrible years, the sufferings of the Protestants of Bohemia and the 'palatinate,' were something unimaginable. The cry reached England, and public help was sought and denied. But it went not everywhere unheard, unheeded. The Puritans, Sibbes among the first, recognised their brotherhood, and out of their own private resources sought to do a little, if it were only to shew their sympathy. I have been fortunate enough to recover a touching memorial of their efforts. Preserved among very different papers in Her Majesty's Record Office is a 'circular' letter, which, in the pathos of its simple words, goes right to the heart. Here it is :—

Whereas, a late information is given to his Matie of the lamentable distresses of two hundred and forty godly preachers, with their wifes and families, and sundrie thousands of godly private persons with them, cast out of their house and homes, out of their callings and countreys, by the furie of the mercilesse papists in the Upper Palatinate, whose heavie condicion is such as they are forced to steale their servises of religion in woods and solitarie places, not without continual feare and damage of their lives ; and whose present want is such as they would be very thankfull for coarse bread (and) drinke if they could gett it. As tenderinge the miserie and want of deare brethren and sisters, desire all godly persons to whom these presents may come, as fellowe feelinge members of the same body of Jesus Christ, to comiserate their present want and enlarge their hearts and hands for some present and private supply for them till some publique means (which hereafter may be hoped) may be raised for their reliefe, assuring themselves that whatsoever is cast into heaven, and falleth into the lappe of Christ in his members, shall return with abundant increase in the harvest ; neither lett any be discouraged least their bounty should miscarrie, for we knowe a sure and safe way whereby whatsoever is given shall undoubtedly come to their hands to (whom) it is intended.

2 Martii 1627.　　　　　　(Signed)　　Tho. Taylor.
　　　　　　　　　　　　　　　　　　　Richard Sibbs.
　　　　　　　　　　　　　　　　　　　John Davenport.
　　　　　　　　　　　　　　　　　　　William Gouge.*

* 'Circular.' Described in 'Calendar of State Papers, Domestic Series of the Reign of Charles I., 1627-28.' By John Bruce, 1858 (Longman).

One of two copies of this affecting ' circular' is endorsed by Laud, and the names noted so carefully, that the Sibbs within is corrected to Sibbes without. One marvels what ground even a Laud could find for opposition, much less persecution, in so piteous an appeal. But when there is a will to hurt or hinder, an occasion is not ill to devise. Perchance the vehement words, ' *merciless papists*,' stung. At any rate, the four honoured men, Richard Sibbes, William Gouge, Thomas Taylor, John Davenport, were summoned before the Star Chamber, and reprimanded. It is not at all wonderful that William Prynne, in his ' Canterburie's Doom,' should ask, ' *By what law of the land*'—a question, by the way, that rings all through the charges of this extraordinary book, like a Gerizzim curse—' did they convert Doctor Gouge, Doctor Sibbes, Doctor Taylor, and Master Davenport, as notorious delinquents, only for setting their hands to a certificate upon entreaty, testifying the distressed condition of some poor ministers of the Palatinate, and furthering a private contribution among charitable Christians for their relief, when public collections failed ?'

It does not appear what further steps, if any, were taken ; but one thing is certain, the miserable persecution did not ' silence' Sibbes. For he not only preached, but published passionately rebuking words against the national lukewarmness. ' What,' asks he, ' shall the members of Christ suffer in other countries, and we profess ourselves to be living members, and *yet not sympathize with them?* We must be conformable to our Head, before we can come to heaven.' * What a pass things had reached, when those in authority would have shut even the hand of private charity against such sufferers ! It is impossible to restrain indignation when reading of James's more than poltroonly, more than mean, desertion of his own ' flesh and blood,' not to speak of Protestantism ; but doubly base was Laud's interference to stamp out as a pestilent thing, this little effort to relieve ' godly preachers and private persons.' It only added to that thunder-cloud, which in a few years was to launch its lightnings on his own head, and whose preluding shadows were even now darkening the sky : such retribution as comes

' When the quick darting lightning's flash
Is the clear glitter of His golden spear.' †

---

* ' Soul's Conflict.'   † Cecil and Mary, by Jackson, p. 19 (1858.)

CHAPTER VIII.

The Preacher of Gray's Inn under surveillance—Controversy not sought by Sibbes
—Loyal to Church and State—The Puritans no 'Schismatics'—Witness-bearing
—Wonder and yet no Wonder—Laud's 'Beauty of Holiness'—'Solemnity'—
Persecution—'Silencing'—William Prynne—Puritan Literature—Laudian-
Bishop's Literature—Sibbes against Popery—Lord Keeper Finch—The 'Im-
propriation' Scheme—Sibbes a 'Feoffee'—Checks upon Laud—'Overthrow'
of 'Feoffees'—Confiscation—Banishment—Verdict upon Laud.

The Star Chamber citation, because of The Palatinate, with its result—a severe reprimand, and treatment as of 'notorious delinquents,'—was only a slighter issue of that unsleeping and vengeful resolution to suppress all Puritanism, which through upwards of a quarter of a century, Laud had planned. Accordingly, though defeated in the matter of the Palatinate, in so far as '*silencing*' Sibbes and his compeers was concerned, they, in common with all the 'good men and true' of the period—for really it appears that every man of note in his day, who was not his creature, was the object of his annoyance—were *watched.** Nor is it at all difficult to understand, that such preaching as was being heard from Sunday to Sunday at 'Gray's Inn,' and down in Cambridge, and by crowds in St Mary's, when reported to him, as everything was reported—must have been superlatively offensive. We do not find Sibbes mixed up with the controversies of the day. There is in his works a noteworthy absence of those fires of intolerant passion that burn so fiercely in many of the writings and actings of his contemporaries. Never once do we meet with him in the ante-chamber of 'the Court,' or mingling with the venal crowds that in unholy rivalry bade high and higher, or more properly low and lower, for place, seeking to cover their 'multitude of sins,' not with charity, but lawn sleeves. He lived serenely apart from the miserable squabbling and personal resentments, and exacerbations of the semi-political, semi-theological polemics that agitated state and church. He was loyal, even tenderly charitable to those in authority ; and true to the church, if only the church would be true to him, by being true to its Head. Let us hear what he was saying about both in those days. Of the State he thus speaks :—'Sometimes it falleth out that those that are under the government of others are most

* 'Watched.' Scattered up and down Sibbes's writings are various indications of his knowledge of this espionage, e. g., 'So in coming to hear the word of God, some come to observe the elegancy of words and phrases, *some to catch advantage, perhaps, against the speaker, men of a devilish temper.*'—('Bowels Opened,' pp. 130–31.)

injurious, by waywardness and harsh censures, herein disparaging and discouraging the endeavours of superiors for public good. In so great weakness of man's nature, and especially in this crazy age of the world, *we ought to take in good part any moderate happiness we enjoy by government ;* and not be altogether as a nail in the wound, exasperating things by misconstruction. *Here love should have a mantle to cast upon the lesser errors of those above us. Oftentimes the poor man is the oppressor by unjust clamours. We should labour to give the best interpretation to the actions of governors that the nature of the actions will possibly bear.'* * Similar sentiments abound. Of the Church we have many wise and considerate words. He had no wish for separation : none of the Puritans had, until they were driven to it. So far from seeking to divide 'the church' and injure it—the refrain of many an accusation—Sibbes has sarcasms that perhaps might have been spared, against those who even then felt they could not remain within her pale. 'Fractions,' he says, with an approach to unkindness very unusual with him, 'always breed factions.' He could not mean it ; but this was capable of being turned by Laud to his own account. He was quick as a sleuth-hound to discern taint of treason. But we have more full and explicit statements. Thus with more than ordinary vehemence he expostulates, accuses :—' What a joyful spectacle is this to Satan and his faction, to see those that are separated from the world fall in pieces among themselves ! Our discord is our enemy's melody. *The more to blame those that for private aims affect differences from others, and will not suffer the wounds of the church to close and meet together.'†*

Was this man, so truly a man of peace, one to track and keep under surveillance, as though he had been at once traitor and fanatic ? Whence came it ? The answer is too easy. Though 'slow to speak,' and sweet-natured to a fault, he was fearless when the occasion demanded it.‡ Even immediately on saying the above,

* Bruised Reed, e. ix.   † Bruised Reed, c. xvii.

‡ 'Sweet-natured to a fault.' Brook ('Lives of the Puritans,' ii. 419) remarks: 'This reverend divine was eminently distinguished for a meek and quiet spirit, being *always unwilling to offend those in power.*' This is too general, for however gentle, Sibbes, when roused, spoke out with no thought of who might be, or might not be, offended. For, says he, 'It argues a base disposition, either for frown or favour, to desert a good cause in evil times' ('Bowels Opened,' 1st edition, 1639, 4to, p. 45). Brook continues, from Calamy (Calamy's Account, vol. ii. pp. 605, 606): 'This trait in his character will appear from the following anecdote: —A fellowship being vacant in Magdalen College, for which Archbishop Laud recommended his bell-ringer at Lambeth, with an evident design of quarrelling with

he takes care to guard himself from misconstruction, by adding :—
' Which must not be understood, as if men should dissemble their
judgment in any truth where there is just cause of expressing themselves ; for the least truth is Christ's, and not ours : and therefore
we are not to take liberty to affirm or deny at our pleasure. There
is a due in a penny, as well as in a pound ; *therefore we must be
faithful in the least truth, when season calleth for it.*' But
again, so gentle and unpolemic was he, he continues finely :—' But
in some cases peace, by keeping our faith to ourselves, Rom. xiv.
22, is of more consequence than the open discovery of some things
we take to be true : *considering the weakness of man's nature is
such, that there can hardly be a discovery of any difference in
opinion, without some estrangement of affection.* So far as men
are not of one mind, they will hardly be of one heart, except where
grace and the peace of God, Col. iii. 15, bear great rule in the heart.
*Therefore, open show of difference is never good but when it is
necessary ;* however some, from a desire to be somebody, turn into
by-ways, and yield to a spirit of contradiction in themselves.'*
And then, Leighton-like, he turns away from the distractions
around him, and thinks of the ' rest that remains.' ' Our blessed
Saviour, when he was to leave the world, what doth he press upon
his disciples more than peace and love ? And in his last prayer,
with what earnestness did he beg of his Father that they might be
one, as he and the Father were one ! John xvii. 21. But what he
prayed for on earth, we shall only enjoy perfectly in heaven. *Let
this make the meditation of that time the more sweet to us.*'†
Even so—

> ' Search well another world ; who studies this,
> Travels in clouds ; seeks manna where none is.' ‡

One wonders, and yet does not wonder, how such a peaceable
and loveable man came to be thus harassed. But what has the
dove done to make the serpent strike its fang into it ? Simply

them if they refused, or of putting a spy upon them if they accepted, Dr Sibbes, who
was ever unwilling to provoke his superiors, told the fellows that Lambeth-house
would be obeyed ; and that the person was young, and might in time prove hopeful.
The fellows therefore consented, and the man was admitted.' This 'anecdote'
carries improbability in the face of it, and neither Calamy nor Brook adduce any
authority. Sibbes could have no voice in ' Magdalen,' in the election or rejection of
a ' fellow.' Nor is there the slightest memorial of such an appointment as is stated.
Surely if it had been made, name and date would have been notorious. Amid the
many charges against Laud, this has no place either in Prynne or elsewhere.
Calamy is not guilty, ordinarily, of introducing mere idle gossip, but it would seem
that in the present instance he has.

* and † Bruised Reed, c. xvii.
‡ Henry Vaughan, Silex Scintillans. Edition by Lyte, 1847, page 17.

MEMOIR OF RICHARD SIBBES, D.D.

crossed its path. What the lamb, to cause the wolf to take it by the throat? Again, simply *crossed its path.* Sibbes had done that with Laud. While the king, under his mitred councillor's tuition, was straining every nerve to un-Sabbath Sunday, Sibbes and his co-Puritans held fast its inviolable authority. While proclamations, unsanctioned by Parliament, were issued to substitute the May-pole for the Cross, the Book of Sports for the Book of God, and the village green for the sanctuary, Sibbes held up the cross and summoned the people to the sanctuary. While all doctrinal preaching, all declarations of the *grace* of God in Jesus Christ, was sought to be put down (precursor of the infamous 'Directions'), Sibbes avouched his Calvinism, and spoke with no bated breath of Arminianism. While *churchmen* of the school of Laud would have men regard transubstantiation as a ' *school nicety,*' bowing to the table of the 'Lord, as '*becoming reverence,*' images in churches worthy ' commemoration,' sacerdotal absolution and confession to a priest as '*proper things,*' the Lord's Supper not as a sacrament, but as a sacrifice,—Sibbes protested, and gave them their proper designa tion, with no periphrasis or courtly phrase, of papistical innovation and delusions of the devil. I am not sure that I would make all his and the Puritans' side-thrusts against ' the papist' my own. I fear I cannot acquit either them or him of ' upbraiding,' and even blameable uncharity for the men, in the honesty of his indignation against their doctrines and measures. But we must not forget the circumstances of ' the time.' He was old enough to remember the Armada, sent to his own Suffolk shore under a pope's blessing, and a ' bull' being nailed to the palace-door with a pope's ban. He was cognizant of innumerable plots, not merely against our religious, but also our civil, liberties. He heard claims asserted, not for equality, but supremacy. And then there were those high in authority, coquetting with that popery that had incarnadined England with her best blood, and had been got rid of at a cost inestimable. He could not but speak, and, speaking as a patriot and Protestant, it was not easy to '*prophesy smooth things.*' Perhaps Laud would have endured Sibbes's bold and passionate rebuke of the prevailing sins of the age, and even, however galled, have winked at his full and fervid assertions of the principles of the reformation from popery, and clear and articulate condemnation of Arminianism, had he gone no further. But words were not only to be answered with words, be it granted unadvised words, with occasional kindredly unadvised words. Action was to be met with action, if ' the church ' were not to be only a masked re-establishment of popery, and if the Calvinism of its fathers were not to degenerate into *ultra*-Arminianism ; and it was done, as we shall see. Peter Heylin was now at the ear of Laud ; and Hacket observes, that ' they that watched the increase of Arminianism, said, confidently, that it was from the year 1628 that the tide of it began to come in , and this because it was from that year that ' all the preferments were cast on one side.' * Similar is the testimony concerning the favour shewn to popery. Thus opposing Laud in his two darling objects, it is easy to foresee that one like Sibbes, resident in London, could not fail to come into conflict with the vigilant and suspicious head of the church. Nor are we to suppose that, if *he* was watched by Lambeth's police, Lambeth went unwatched. How far the primate was going in his ' papistical tendencies,' may be gathered from one notorious exhibition. Besides its bearing on the persecution springing out of the impropriation scheme, it gives point to a suggestive hit by Sibbes, which was probably the thing that stung Laud to further action against him and his coadjutors in another blessed work. I therefore give the record of it from the admittedly authoritative pages of Rushworth and Wharton, *in extenso :*—On Sunday the 16th of January 1630–1, a new church—St Catherine Creed—in Leadenhall Street, was consecrated. It had been re-built, and had been suspended by the primate from all divine service, sermons or sacraments, until it should be re-consecrated. Laud and a number of his clergy came in the morning to perform the ceremony. Then as strange and sad a ' performance' as ever men beheld was enacted, regard being had to the fact that the performer was the Protestant Primate of England :—

' At the bishop's approach to the west door,' says Rushworth, ' some that were prepared for it cried, with a loud voice, " Open, open, ye everlasting doors, that the king of glory may enter in !" ' and presently the doors were opened, and the bishop, with some doctors, and many other principal men, went in, and immediately, falling down upon his knees, with his eyes lifted up, and his arms spread abroad, uttered these words : " This place is holy ; the ground is holy : in the name of the Father, Son, and Holy Ghost, I pronounce it holy." Then he took up some of the dust, and threw it up into the air, several times, in his going up towards the chancel. † When they approached near to the rail and communion-table, the bishop bowed towards it several times ; and, returning, they went round the church in procession, saying the 100th Psalm, and after that the 19th Psalm, and then said a form of prayer, commencing, "Lord Jesus

* Hacket . . . Life of Williams, Lord Keeper. Pt. ii. p. 42 and p. 82.

† Masson. ' Life of Milton,' i. 350, adds here this foot-note :—This was sworn to on Laud's trial by two witnesses; but Laud denies it, and moreover, says that, if it had been true, it would not have been a popish ceremony, as the Romish pontifical prescribes, not ' dust,' but ' ashes' to be thrown up on such occasions.

Christ," &c., and concluding, " We consecrate this church, and separate it unto thee, as holy ground, not to be profaned any more to common use." After this, the bishop being near the communion-table, and taking a written book in his hand (a copy, as was afterwards alleged, of a form in the Romish pontifical, but according to Laud, furnished him by the deceased Bishop Andrewes), pronounced curses upon those that should afterwards profane that holy place by musters of soldiers, or keeping profane law-courts, or carrying burdens through it ; and at the end of every curse, bowed towards the east, and said, "Let all the people say, Amen." When the curses were ended, he pronounced a number of blessings upon all those that had any hand in framing and building of that sacred and beautiful church, and those that had given, or should hereafter give, any chalices, plate, ornaments, or utensils ; and at the end of every blessing, he bowed towards the east, and said, "Let all the people say, Amen." After this followed the sermon, which being ended, the bishop consecrated and administered the sacrament in manner following :—As he approached the communion-table, he made several lowly bowings ; and coming up to the side of the table, where the bread and wine were covered, he bowed seven times ; and then, after the reading of many prayers, he came near the bread, and gently lifted up a corner of the napkin wherein the bread was laid ; and when he beheld the bread, he laid it down again, flew back a step or two, bowed three several times towards it, then he drew near again, and opened the napkin, and bowed as before. Then he laid his hand on the cup, which was full of wine, with a cover upon it, which he let go again, went back, and bowed thrice towards it ; then he came near again, and lifting up the cover of the cup, looked into it, and seeing the wine, let fall the cover again, retired back, and bowed as before. Then he received the sacrament, and gave it to some principal men ; after which, many prayers being said, the solemnity of the consecration ended.'

That was the sort of thing that the primate and his like-minded bishops, sought to impose on men as 'SOLEMNITY !' That '*mounte-bank* holiness' (it is Sir Philip Sidney's word of scorn) was to be its translation of the grand old ' Beauty of Holiness,' (1 Chron. xvi. 29 ; Ps. xxix. 2, and xcvi. 9).* It is no light occasion that

---

* 'Beauty of holiness.' The vehement words of John Milton, stern as Jeremiah, a few year later, are memorable, and may not be passed by :—' Now for their demeanour within the church, how have they disfigur'd and defac't that more than angelick brightnes, the unclouded serenity of Christian religion, *with the dark over-casting of superstitious coaps and flaminical vestures.* . . . Tell me. ye priests, wherefore this gold, wherefore these roabs and surplices, over the gospel? Is our religion guilty of the first trespasse, and hath need of cloathing to cover her nakednesse? What does this else but cast an ignominey upon the perfection of Christ's ministery by seeking to adorn it with that which was the poor remedy of our shame ? Believe it, wondrous doctors, *all corporeal resemblances of inward holinesse and beauty are now past.*' (The Reason of Church Government, B. II. ch. ii. p. 154. Mitford's Milton. Prose Works, vol. i. Pickering.) Elsewhere, denouncing the 'chaff of over-dated ceremonies,' he thus describes the Laudian 'prelaty :'—'They began to draw down all the divine intercourse betwixt God and the soul, yea, the very shape of God himself, into an exterior and bodily form, urgently pretending a necessity and obligement of joining the body in a formal reverence and worship circumscribed : they hallowed it, they fumed it, they sprinkled it, they bedecked it, not in robes of

calls for one's judgment of another in so awful and sacred a thing as his religion, however it may be darkened by superstition, or lightened by the fires of the wildest fanaticism. Deplorable, therefore, as this mummery may be to us, we may not pronounce that it was an unreal, much less that it was a farcical thing to its chief actor. Such a soul as his, so small, so narrow, may have found channel deep enough for its reverence in such return upon an effete ritualism. We may agree with Macaulay's epithet of 'imbecile,' but not with the Puritan's angry charge of 'hypocrite.' But when one realises that prison, fine, the knife, the shears, persecution to the death, were the award of every honest soul that refused to regard as the 'Beauty of Holiness' such exaggerations of even popery, it is hard to withhold an anathema, ringing as Paul's, on the memory of him who devised, and of the craven bishops who cravenly enforced them. There the spider-soul sat, in its craft, spreading out its net-work over broad England, and by its Harsnets and Curles, Mountagus and Buckridges, Bancrofts and Wrens, and Mainwarings, united in a brotherhood of evil, sought to entrap all who held to the divine simplicity of the New Testament. The secret threads, revealed by the tears of the persecuted, as by the morning dew is revealed the drop-spangled and else concealed web of the open-air spider, thrilled news up to the hand that grasped all, and forth the fiat went. 'Within a single year, at this period,' says Neal, 'many lecturers were put down, and such as preached against Arminianism or the new ceremonies were suspended and silenced, among whom were the Rev. Mr John Rogers of Dedham, Mr Daniel Rogers of Wethersfield, Mr Hooker of Chelmsford, Mr White of Knightsbridge, Mr Archer, Mr William Martin, Mr Edwards, Mr Jones, Mr Dod, Mr Hildersam, Mr Ward, Mr Saunders, Mr James Gardiner, Mr Foxley, and many others.' *

We have the burning words of Prynne, that at a 'later day,' in the day of his humiliation, the primate had to meet. Thus forcibly is the charge put—nor was it ever touched :—

'As he thus preferred Popish and Arminian clergymen to the chief eccle-

pure innocency, but of pure linen, with other deformed and fantastic dresses, in palls and mitres, gold and gewgaws, fetched from Aaron's old wardrobe or the flamen's vestry ; then was the priest sent to con his motions and his postures, his liturgies and lurries, till the soul, by this means of overbodying herself, given up to fleshly delights, bated her wing apace downwards.' In our own day, one has characterised the same phenomenon, as presented by Tractarianism, which, indeed, was the harvest of the baleful seed sown by Laud, as 'a thing of flexions and genuflexions, postures and impostures, with a dash of man-millinery.'

* Hist. of Puritans, Vol. i. p. 589, &c. (ed., 3 vols. 8vo, 1837.)

siastical preferments in our church, so, on the contrary, (following the counsel of Cautzen, the Mogonutive Jesuit, in his politics, see ' Look about you '), he discountenanced, suspended, silenced, suppressed, censured, imprisoned, persecuted most of the prime, orthodox, diligent preaching ministers of the realm, and forced many of them to fly into America, Holland, and other foreign places, to avoid his fury, only for opposing his popish innovations, and expressing their fears of the change of our religion. Not to trouble you with any forementioned instances of Mr Peter Smart, Mr Henry Burton, Mr Snelling, and others, we shall instance in some fresh examples. . . . .' Mr Samuel Ward's case, and Mr Chauncy's case, are then narrated. 'To these we could add,' he proceeds, 'Mr Cotton, Mr Hooker, Mr Davenport, Mr Wells, Mr Peters, Mr Glover, and sundry other ministers, driven into New England and other plantations.' And then ' Dr Stoughton, *Dr Sibbes*, Dr Taylor, Dr Gouge, Mr White of Dorchester, Mr Rogers of Dedham, with sundry more of our most eminent preaching, orthodox divines, were brought into the High Commission, and troubled or silenced for a time by his procurement upon frivolous pretences, but in truth because they were principal props of our Protestant religion against his Popish and Arminian innovations.' *

Now, we have the actual books containing the actual preaching of these men, and the numerous others who shared their persecution. They are in our libraries ; and he must be either a bold or a very foolish man, not only rash, but reckless, who gainsays that, *remove these books from the Christian literature of the period and you remove the very life-blood of that literature.*

The most recent, truthful, and catholic of ' the church' historians, Mr Perry,† admits that all the practical writers of the age were of the Puritans and sufferers for nonconformity; and he names a few, Willet and Dyke, Preston and Byfield, Bolton and Hildersam, and Sibbes. ' This fact,' he candidly observes, 'must needs have told with extreme force against the interests of the church. It was doubtless alleged that the church divines could only speak when their position or their order was menaced, but in the face of the great and crying sins and scandals of the age they were dumb and tongue-tied ;' and he might have added, in view also of the gross ignorance and darkness in which whole districts of the country were shrouded.

I should make larger reservation or exceptions in favour of 'church' writers than Mr Perry does ; for I find in Thomas Adams and Anthony Farindon, and others, whom I love equally with the foremost of the Puritans, the same preaching with theirs. Still it remains that the men whom Laud delighted to honour were the men who were vehement enough to bring men to ' the church,' but not at all concerned about bringing them to Christ ; ready to dispense

* ' Canterburie's Doom,' pp. 362, *seq.* 1646, folio.
† The History of the Church of England from the death of Elizabeth to the present time. By the Rev. G. G. Perry, M.A., Rector of Waddington. Vol. I. 1861. (Saunders. Otley, & Co.) See C. ix. p. 326.

the sacraments, but oblivious of their antitype; swift to jangle in hot controversies on 'super-elementation,' but cold about the one transcendent change; reverers of the altar, but despisers of the cross. We have defences of the church, its tithes and dignities, its upholstery and repairs, *ad nauseam*. We have the primate himself fervid about his genu-flexions and reverence to the *name* of Christ, and the name only; and a Mountagu, ribald as Billingsgate against holy Samuel Ward. They were, as was jested of a modern Lord Chancellor, buttresses rather than pillars of 'the church.' We look in vain all through the extant writings of the bishops named, from Laud downward, for anything approaching one earnest, heartfelt utterance as from a servant of Jesus Christ to perishing sinners, one living word to men as 'under wrath,' nay, for one flash of genius, one gush of human feeling. They had no answer for the 'Anxious Inquirer' as he cried—

> 'I am a sinner, full of doubts and fears,
> Make me a humble thing of love and tears.' *

There exists not a more meagre, inane, contemptible literature, taken as a whole, than that composed of the Laudian books *proper;* for it were a historic blunder, as well as a slander, to include Hall or Ussher or Bedell or Davenant among them, from the mere accident of their first appointment, more or less, coming from Laud. Yet we must believe that what they printed and gave to the world was their best, and at least was the preaching their auditories heard. On the other hand, it equally remains unchallengeable that the men whom Laud delighted to persecute were the only men then in England who were really discharging, in the fear of God, their office of preachers of the gospel, men, at the same time, of generous loyalty, and lovers, with the deepest affection, of that reformed church from which they were driven in 1662.

Such having been the state of things, it is only what we should expect, to find even the unpolemic and gentle Sibbes speaking out against the doings and tendencies of the men in authority. There is a time to be silent, *and* a time to speak. Fealty to truth demanded plain words, and translating of words into acts. Nor was either awanting. For words take these, over which we can conceive even the rheumy eyes of the primate flashing fire. They are taken from sermons preached during this period, and afterwards fearlessly published. I venture to italicise some few lines :—

'What spirit shall we think them to be of that take advantages of the bruised-ness and infirmities of men's spirits to relieve them with false peace for

---

* Hartley Coleridge, Poems, ii. p. 387 (edition 1851).

their own worldly ends? A wounded spirit will part with anything. Most of the gainful points of popery, as confession, satisfaction, merit, purgatory, &c., spring from hence, but they are physicians of no value, or rather tormentors than physicians at all. *It is a greater blessing to be delivered from " the sting of these scorpions" than we are thankful for.* Spiritual *tyranny is the greatest tyranny,* and then especially when it is where most mercy should be shewed; yet even there some, like cruel surgeons, delight in making long cures, to serve themselves upon the misery of others. It bringeth men under a terrible curse, " when they will not remember to shew mercy, but persecute the poor and needy man, that they might even slay the broken in heart," Ps. cix. 16.

' Likewise, to such as raise temporal advantage to themselves out of the spiritual misery of others, join such as raise estates by betraying the church, *and are unfaithful in the trust committed unto them,* when the CHILDREN SHALL CRY FOR THE BREAD OF LIFE, AND THERE IS NONE TO GIVE THEM, *bringing thus upon the people of God that heavy judgment* of a spiritual famine, starving Christ in his members. Shall we so requite so good a Saviour, who counteth the love and mercy shewed in " feeding his lambs," John xxi. 15, as shewed to himself?

' Last of all, they carry themselves very unkindly towards Christ, who stumble at this his low stooping unto us in his GOVERNMENT and ORDINANCES, that are *ashamed of the simplicity of the gospel,* that count preaching foolishness.

' They, out of the pride of their heart, think they may do well enough without the help of the WORD and SACRAMENTS, and think CHRIST TOOK NOT STATE ENOUGH UPON HIM, AND THEREFORE THEY WILL MEND THE MATTER WITH THEIR OWN DEVICES, whereby they may give the better content to flesh and blood, *as in popery.'* *

Elsewhere, in his most eloquent sermon entitled ' The Saint's Safety in Evil Times,' he thus fearlessly speaks:—

' I beseech you consider, what hurt have we ever had by the " Reformation" of religion? Hath it come naked unto us? Hath it not been attended with peace and prosperity? Hath God been " a barren wilderness to us?" Jer. ii. 31. Hath not God been a wall of fire about us? which if he had not been, it is not the water that compasseth our island could have kept us.†

Once more, in the ' Ungodly's Misery,' also ' preached ' at this period, we have these plain-spoken words:—

' What is the gospel but salvation and redemption by Christ *alone!* Therefore, Rome's church is an apostate church, and may well be styled an adulteress and a whore, because she is fallen from her husband Christ Jesus. And what may we think of those that would bring light and darkness, Christ and Antichrist, the ark and Dagon, together, that would reconcile us, as if it were no great matter?'‡

Still again, in his exceeding precious sermons on Canticles, he strikes high, even right at the prelates, on their neglect of abounding error:—

' Thus,' says he, ' popery grew up *by degrees,* till it overspread the

* ' Bruised Reed,' page 77.   ‡ ' Ungodly's Misery,' p. 388.

† ' Saint's Safety,' page 312.

church, *whilst the watchmen that should have kept others awake* FELL ASLEEP THEMSELVES. And thus we answer the papists when they quarrel with us about the beginning of their errors. They ask of us when such and such an heresy began; we answer, THAT THOSE THAT SHOULD HAVE OBSERVED THEM WERE ASLEEP. Popery is a " mystery," that *crept into the church by degrees* UNDER GLORIOUS PRETENCES. *Their errors had modest beginnings.*'

These two words, ' glorious pretences,' must have been treasured up by Laud. They reappear in his ' Answers ' to the ' Charges ' against him, as I shall notice anon.

These were fiery words, and given to the world in print, the former in ' The Bruised Reed,' in 1629–30, the latter in ' The Saint's Safety,' in 1632–3, they could not fail to rouse the primate. Almost immediately upon his appointment to the preachership of Gray's Inn, Laud had sought to have him deprived and silenced ; for tidings had reached him of the Trinity lectureship and the evangelical 'soul-fatting' (good old Bolton's word) preaching there. But Lord Keeper Finch had interfered to defeat his machinations, a right good service by not the best of men I fear, which he did not forget to plead when he stood at the bar of the House. Thus did he bring it up, the little quarto containing the full ' speech ' being now before me :—' I hope for my affection in religion no man doubteth me. What my education was, and under whom I lived for many yeares, is well knowne. I lived neere thirty years in the society of Gray's Inne ; and if one (that was a reverend preacher there in my time, Doctor Sibs) were now living, he were able to give testimony to this House that when a party ill-affected in religion sought to tyre and weary him out, he had his chiefest encouragement and help from me.' Let the erring Lord Keeper have the benefit of this redeeming trait.

Defeated in this earlier effort, Laud postponed, but did not abandon, his purpose. He soon found a pretext. As was observed before, Sibbes was a man of beneficent action as well as of beneficent words ; and holding as he did that the church was for the nation, and not the nation for the church,—that the ministry was for the preaching of the gospel,—he joined hand and heart in counterworking those schemes, that, by quenching every ' golden candlestick ' within which burned the oil of the sanctuary, sought to bring back the darkness and superstitions of the worst of popish times. Things had come to the crisis of endurance. If Laud and his myrmidons would ' deprive,' ' out,' ' silence,' ' persecute ' the humble, faithful, godly preachers of salvation by grace, who were bearing the ' beat and burden ' of work, and would intrude men, from the bishop to his humblest curate, who enforced a thinly-veiled popery in practice, and *un*scriptural, *anti*scriptural teaching in doctrine, something was demanded that should neutralise such doings. What was devised is matter of history. 'Feoffees' were appointed—the sacred 'twelve' in number—to raise funds, and buy in from time to time such 'impropriations' as were in the hands of laymen, when they could be purchased, and then to appoint therein as lecturers those who would really do the work of preaching. Superadded was the appointment of similar lecturers in the more neglected regions where lay-impropriations were not purchasable. Years before Sibbes had expressed his earnest wish that a 'lecturer' were in every dark corner of England.* It was a noble enterprise, and was nobly responded to. The best and wisest, the purest and holiest men of the age, took their part in the undertaking. I hesitate not to avouch, that there was scarcely a man whose name is now remembered for good, but was found subscribing amply and co-operating zealously for its accomplishment. The national heart was stirred, and it was found to beat in the right place. Sibbes, along with his old friends and coadjutors, Davenport and Gouge, was appointed one of the 'Feoffees.'. It needs not to be told how this drew down the vengeance of Laud. The scheme had been more or less hindered from its inauguration in 1626, but not till 1632–3 (coincident with Sibbes's defences of 'The Re‑ formation from Popery') was open action taken. The delay was caused by no relenting, much less forgetfulness. But events in the interval had transpired to 'give pause.' James had died, and his son reigned in his stead. The plague had passed over the metropolis in 1625, and there was 'lamentation and woe' in tens of thousands of households, again returning dolefully in 1630. There were political movements, also, that whitened to pallor the proudest cheek. One 'Mr Cromwell' had come up to Parliament in 1627–8. Besides 'the Petition of Right,' and the extorted and memorable *Soit fait comme il est desiré*, and the 'Declaration,' most uncourtly words fell from Masters Pym and Hampden and Eliot, and many others. But very especially was there plain-speaking, in his own stammering but forcible and resolute fashion, by 'Mr Cromwell' about increase of 'popery.' The House of Commons resolved itself into a Committee of Religion. Let Thomas Carlyle, tell the issue. 'It was,' says he, 'on the 11th day of February 1628–9, that Mr Cromwell, member for

---

* His words are memorable : 'If it were possible, it were to be wished that there were set up some lights in all the dark corners of this kingdom, that might shine to those people that sit in darkness and in the shadow of death.'—(Saint's Safety, p. 331 of the present volume.)

Huntingdon (then in his thirtieth year), stood up and made his first speech, a fragment of which has found its way into history, and is now known to all mankind. He said : "He had heard by relation from one Dr Beard (his old schoolmaster at Huntingdon) that Dr Alabaster (prebendary of St Paul's and rector of a parish in Herts) had preached flat popery at Paul's Cross ; and that the Bishop of Winchester (Dr Neile) had commanded him, as his diocesan, he should preach nothing to the contrary. Mainwaring, so justly censured in this House for his sermons, was, by the same bishop's means, preferred to a rich living. If these are the steps to church-preferment, what are we to expect?"' * We shall probably not greatly err if we conclude that even the 'red face' of Laud blanched under that question of 'Mr Cromwell,' knowing as he well did that the facts named were only two out of many, and knowing also the 'stuff' of which the men were made who were upon the inquisition. Then came 'remonstrances' and 'declarations' stronger still, and they who drew them up meant to have what they demanded. True, the chief speakers were 'indicted' in the Star-Chamber, and ultimately sent to the Tower, 'Mr Cromwell,' and 'Mr Pym,' and 'Mr Hampden' alone excepted (marvellous and suggestive exceptions). There lay Denzil Holles and Sir John Eliot, John Selden, Benjamin Valentine, and William Couton, Sir Miles Hobart and William Longe, William Strode and Sir Peter Hayman. For eleven years it was decreed to be penal so much as to speak of assembling another Parliament. There were 'wars and rumours of wars,' too. Every one who at all knows the time can see that a constraint which could not be disregarded was put upon Laud in the matter of his persecuting for religion. He durst not go in the teeth of the unmistakeable menaces of the last memorable Parliament. He noted down everything, and certainly would not fail to note down what Rous and Pym, Eliot and Selden, had said. Let us hear a little of what was said. Francis Rous, trembling like an old Hebrew prophet with his 'burden,' had denounced that 'error of Arminianism which makes the grace of God lackey it after the will of man,' and called on the House to postpone questions of goods and liberties to this question, which concerned 'eternal life, men's souls, yea, God himself.' Sir John Eliot repudiated the claim that 'the bishops and clergy alone should interpret church doctrine ; and, professing his respect for some bishops, declared that there were others, *and two especially*, from whom nothing orthodox could come, and to empower whom to interpret *would be the ruin of national religion.*' John Selden, grave and calm, referred to individual cases in which

* Cromwell's Letters and Speeches, 8d edition, i. 29.

Popish and Arminian books were allowed, while Calvinistic books were restrained, notwithstanding that there was no law in England to prevent the printing of any books, but only a decree in Star-Chamber.' And then on one occasion the whole House stood up together, and vowed a vow against '*innovations in the faith.*' The issue of that, passed with closed doors, and with clenching of teeth and gripping of sword-hilts, none will soon forget. We have to do with only one of the three 'Resolutions :—'Whoever shall bring in innovation of religion, or by favour or countenance seem to extend Popery or Arminianism, or other opinion disagreeing from the true and orthodox church, shall be reputed a capital enemy to this kingdom and commonwealth.' *

After these things it is remarkable that the king, a man without mind, and Laud, a man without either mind or heart, should at all have adventured to go against the mind and heart of England. But so it was. There was of necessity greater secrecy, very much of covert plotting against the liberties, civil and religious, of England. The 'feoffees' at last, borne with involuntarily from 1626, were summoned before the Star Chamber and High Commission both. And that was but the execution of Laud's cherished purpose from the beginning. For in that strangest of strange 'Diaries,' the oddest combination, that ever has been written, of piety and grovelling superstition, of faith and the most babyish credulity, (for Pepys' is wisdom itself in comparison †), we light upon this entry :—

' Things which I have projected to do, if God bless me in them—
' III. To overthrow the feoffment, dangerous both to Church and State, going under the specious pretence of buying in impropriations.'

Opposite these words, a few out of many equally deplorable, that a little onward came to be to their writer terrible as the mystic 'handwriting' of Babylon's palace-wall, is inscribed 'DONE.' And it was *done*—for the moment; but it was a tremendous success to its doer. If only Nemesis had been touched with ruth to blot out the handwriting ! But no ! There the entry stood, when perhaps not altogether lawfully or honourably, at least not courteously, the diary was seized :—

* Consult for the facts introduced Masson's Life of Milton, i. 181, 829, *seq.*; Carlyle's ' Cromwell;' John Forster's ' Statesmen of the Commonwealth,' and others of his historical works about this period.

† Pepys. I do not know if his prescient entry in favour of the Puritans has been remarked. Having witnessed Ben Jonson's ' Bartholomew Fair,' he jots down, ' And is an excellent play; the more I see it the more I love the wit of it ; *only the business of abusing the Puritans* begins to grow stale, and of no use, *they being the people that at last will be found the wisest.*' See Index of any edition of ' Diary' under ' Bartholomew Fair.'

'Feb. 13. 1632.

' *Wednesday.*—The feoffes that pretended to buy in impropriations were dissolved in the Chequer Chamber. *They were the main instruments for the Puritan faction to undo the Church.* THE CRIMINAL PART RESERVED.'*

Reserved! Ay, and transferred!

Those who had engaged in the impropriation scheme, including Sibbes, having been thus summoned before the Star-Chamber, were dealt with, not as honourable and good men, but as 'criminals and traitors.' The verdict was—CONFISCATION of the funds and BANISHMENT of the men! Some fled to Holland, some to New England.† Had the nation's

* Laud's 'Works,' vol. iii. p. 216, 217.

† Of the 'fugitives' associated with Sibbes in the 'feoffees' scheme, the most eminent was John Davenport. In Anderson's Life of Lady Mary Vere, in ' Memorable Women of Puritan Times,' some very touching letters of his are given from the Brit. Museum MSS. (Birch 4275, No. 69). Two extracts will shew the anxiety in which these godly men were kept, and at the same time shew how far they were from wishing to be ' schismatics,' or in any way to injure the church. First of all, while he and Sibbes and others were under the ban of the ' High Commission' as mentioned above, he writes, ' I have had divers purposes of writing to your honour, only I delayed in hope to write somewhat concerning the event and success of our High Commission troubles ; but I have hoped in vain, for to this day we are in the same condition as before, delayed till the finishing of the session in Paliament, which now is unhappily concluded without any satisfying contentment to the king or commonwealth. *Threatenings were speedily revived against us by the new Bishop of London, Dr Laud, even the next day after the conclusion of the session.* We now expect a fierce storm from the enraged spirits of the two bishops ; ours, as I am informed, hath a particular aim at me upon a former quarrel, so that I expect ere long to be deprived of my pastoral charge in Coleman Street. But I am in God's hand, not in theirs, to whose good pleasure I do contentedly and cheerfully submit myself.'

A more beautiful charity, or more modest assertion of conscience, than in our next extract, can scarcely be imagined.

' Be not troubled, much less discouraged, good madam, at any rumours you meet with concerning my present way. The persecution of the tongue is more fierce and terrible than that of the hand. At this time I have sense of both. . . . . . The truth is, I have not forsaken my ministry, nor resigned up my place, *much less separated from the church*, but am only absent a while to wait upon God, upon the settling and quieting of things, for light to discover my way, being willing to lie and die in prison, if the cause may be advantaged by it, but choosing rather to preserve the liberty of my person and ministry for the service of the church elsewhere, *if all doors are shut against me here.* . . . . . . The only cause of all my present sufferings is the alteration of my judgment in matters of conformity to the ceremonies established, whereby I cannot practise them as formerly I have done ; *wherein I do not censure those that do conform (nay, I account many of them faithful and worthy instruments of God's glory ;* and I know that I did conform with as much inward peace as now I do forbear ; in both my uprightness was the same, but my light different). In this action I walk by that light which shineth into me. . . . . . With much advice of many ministers of eminent note and worth, I have done all that I have done hitherto, and with desire of pitching upon that way wherein God might be most glorified. In his due time he will manifest its truth.'

tongue not been cut out—no Parliament sat for years!—there had been stormy debates on that!

So far as Sibbes was concerned, it does not appear that any part of the sentence was ever put into execution. He continued preacher at Gray's Inn, and Master of Catharine Hall. This assures us that powerful friends, the Brooks and Veres, Manchesters and Warwicks, must have stood by him. But there was no compromise on his part. I find that almost like a menace, and most surely a defiance, Sibbes introduced into a sermon, preached immediately after the decision, an explicit eulogy of Sherland, the recorder of Northampton, for what he had done toward the impropriation scheme ; and published the sermon.*

Still it was crushed, the 'monies' confiscated,* the 'purchases' reversed, the whole holy enterprise branded, and its agents disgraced. One thing is to be recalled. Among the 'things projected,' Laud enumerates, with imbecile forgetfulness, precisely such a scheme of purchase of 'impropriations'—by HIMSELF.† So that it stands confessed that not the thing itself was dangerous and illegal, but the doers of it. Let only him and his appoint to the places, and all was well and right. But let men such as Sibbes, Gouge, Taylor, Davenport in the Church, and the foremost men for worth in the State, their enemies themselves being witnesses, be the appointers, and instantly it smells of 'treason, stratagem, wiles.' These or those dangerous to Church and State ? What is the award of posterity ? And yet defenders have been found for the transparently mendacious and infamous act. Such jeer at the paltry minority of Puritanism, oblivious of what a living poet has finely expressed—

> '. . . . . You trust in numbers, I
> Trust in One only.' ‡

Let us see how Laud himself met it when it came in awful resurrection back upon him. Every one is aware that the suppression of the 'feoffment-impropriation' scheme formed one of the counts in the great roll of accusation, whose issue was the block on Tower Hill. A careful record was kept of charges and answers, and the whole have been republished in the Works of Laud. It is but fitting that what he had to say should appear. Here, then, are 'charge' and 'defence.' The whole case, so vital as between Laud and the Puritan worthies, among whom Richard Sibbes was prominent, can then be judged of :—

* See 'Christ is Best,' in the present volume, p. 349.
† See the whole list in his works, as after-referenced.
‡ Cecil and Mary, as *ante*, p. 10.

That whereas divers gifts and dispositions of divers sums of money were heretofore made by divers charitable and well-disposed persons, for the buying in of divers impropriations, for the maintenance of preaching the word of God in several churches; the said archbp., about eight years last past, wilfully and maliciously caused the said gifts, feoffments, and conveyances, made to the uses aforesaid, to be overthrown in his majesty's Court of Exchequer, contrary to law, as things dangerous to the Church and State, under the specious pretence of buying in appropriations; whereby that pious work was suppressed and trodden down, to the great dishonour of God and scandal of religion.
This article is only about the feoffments. That which I did was this: I was (as then advised upon such information as was given me) clearly of opinion, that this was a cunning way, under a glorious pretence, to overthrow the church government, by getting into their power more dependency of the clergy than the king, and all the peers, and all the bishops in all the kingdom had. And I did conceive the plot the more dangerous for the fairness of the pretence; and that to the State as well as the Church. Hereupon, not "maliciously" (as 'tis charged in the article), but conscientiously, I resolved to suppress it, if by law it might be done. Upon this, I acquainted his majesty with the thing, and the danger which I conceived would in few years spring out of it. The king referred me to his attorney, and the law. Mr Attorney Noye, after some pause upon it, proceeded in the exchequer, and there it was, by judicial proceeding and sentence, overthrown. If this sentence were according to law and justice, then there's no fault at all committed. If it were against law, the fault, whate'er it be, was the judges', not mine; for I solicited none of them. And here I humbly desired, that the Lords would at their leisure read over the sentence given in the exchequer,* which I then delivered in; but by reason of the length, it was not then read. Whether after it were, I cannot tell. I desired likewise that my counsel might be heard in this and all other points of law.

1. The first witness was Mr Kendall.† He says, that speaking with me about Presteen, 'I thanked God that I had overthrown this foeffment.'
2. The second witness, Mr Miller,‡ says he heard me say, 'They would have undone the church, but I have overthrown their feoffment.' These two witnesses prove no more than I confess. For in the manner aforesaid, I deny not but I did my best in a legal way to overthrow it. And if I did thank God for it, it was my duty to do so, the thing being in my judgment so pernicious as it was.
3. The third witness was Mr White, one of the feoffees.§ He says, 'that coming as counsel in a cause before me, when that business was done, I fell bitterly on him as an underminer of the church.' I remember well his coming to me as counsel about a benefice. And 'tis very likely I spake my conscience to him, as freely as he did his to me; but the particulars I remember not; nor do I remember his coming afterwards to me to

* Sir Leolin Jenkins hath a copy of it out of the records of the exchequer. W. S. A. C. (See Rushworth's Collections, vol. ii. pp. 151, 152.)
† 'William Kendall.'—Prynne's Cant. Doom, p. 388.
‡ 'Tempest Miller.'—Ibid.
§ John White. He was, in 1640, M.P. for Southwark, and chairman of the Committee for Religion. He was commonly called 'Century' White from the title of his celebrated tractate, 'The First Century of Malignant Priests,' (Wood. Ath. Ox. iii. 144, 145).

Fulham; nor his offer ' to change the men or the course, so the thing might stand.' For to this I should have been as willing as he was; and if I remember right, there was order taken for this in the decree of the Exchequer. And his majesty's pleasure declared, that no penny so given should be turned to other use. And I have been, and shall ever be, as ready to get in impropriations, by any good and legal way, as any man (as may appear by my labours about the impropriations in Ireland). But this way did not stand either with my judgment or conscience.

1. First, because little or nothing was given by them to the present incumbent, to whom the tithes were due, if to any; that the parishioners which payed them, might have the more cheerful instruction, the better hospitality, and more full relief for their poor.

' 2. Secondly, because most of the men they put in, were persons disaffected to the discipline, if not the doctrine, too, of the Church of England.

' 3. Thirdly, because no small part was given to schoolmasters, to season youth *above*, for their party; and to young students in the universities, to purchase them and their judgments to their side, against their coming abroad into the church.

' 4. Fourthly, because all this power to breed and maintain a faction, was in the hands of twelve men, who were they never so honest, and free from thoughts of abusing this power, to fill the church with schism, yet who should be successors, and what use should be made of the power, was out of human reach to know.'

5. Because this power was assumed by, and not to themselves, without any legal authority, as Mr Attorney assured me.

He further said, ' that the impropriations of Presteen, in Radnorshire, was specially given to St Antolin's, in London.* I say the more the pity, considering the poorness of that country, and the little preaching that was among that poor people, and the plenty which is in London. Yet because it was so given, there was care taken after the decree, that they of St Antolin's had consideration, and I think to the full. He says, ' that indeed they did not give anything to the present incumbents, till good men came to be in their places.' Scarce one incumbent was bettered by them. And what then? In so many places not one ' good man' found? ' Not one factious enough against the church, for Mr White to account him good?' Yet he thinks ' I disposed these things afterwards to unworthy men.' ' Truly, had they been at my disposal, I should not wittingly have given them to Mr White's worthies.' But his majesty laid his command upon his attorney, and nothing was done or to be done in these things, but by his direction. For Dr Heylin, if he spake anything amiss concerning this feoffment, in any sermon of his† he is living to answer it; me it concerns not. ' Mr Brown in the sum of the charge omitted not this. And I answered as before. And in his reply he

---

* This impropriation was, after the forfeiture, granted by King Charles I. to the rector of Presteign for ever. This grant was revoked during the Rebellion, but confirmed by King Charles II. at the beginning of his reign.

† The Sermon to which reference is here made, was preached by Heylin, at St Mary's, Oxford, July 11. 1630, at the Act. The passage relating to the feoffees will be found in Prynne (Cant. Doom, p. 386), who transcribed it from a MS. copy of the Sermon in Abp. Laud's study; and in Heylin (Cypr. Ang. p. 199, Lond. 1671). who appears in his turn to have transcribed it from Prynne.

turned again upon it, that it must be a crime in me, because I projected to overthrow it. But, under favour, this follows not. For to project (though the word 'projector' sounds ill in England), is no more than to forecast and forelay any business. Now as 'tis lawful for me, by all good and fit means, to project the settlement of anything that is good; so is it as lawful, by good and legal means, to project the overthrow of anything that is cunningly or apparently evil. And such did this feoffment appear to my understanding, and doth still.' As for reducing of impropriations to their proper use, they may see (if they please) in my Diary (whence they had this) another project to buy them into the church's use. For given they will not be. But Mr Pryn would shew nothing, nor Mr Nicolas see anything, but what they thought would make against me.

Of this Defence, it must be said in the apophthegm of Helps, 'It would often be as well to condemn a man unheard, as to condemn him upon the reasons which he openly avows for any course of action.'* Still, in common with the whole of the 'Answers,' as tragically told in the 'History of the Troubles,'† it exhibits no little astuteness and dexterity, and more than all his resoluteness in assertion of conscience. There is also characteristic strategy shewn in his retreats behind others who acted with him, now Attorney-General Noye, and now the king himself, with an almost humorous contrast in the surrender of Heylin to his fate. While then we cannot altogether deny that an answer (not reply merely, but answer) is returned, nor that his infamy was shared; yet there lies behind all the indisputable fact, that here was an association of the very salt of Church and State, seeking from their own resources to purchase in a legal way,—in the very way their accuser himself had done, and still proposed to do,—'impropriations' in the hands of laymen who were not only willing, but wishful, to part with them, and to place therein, through the recognised authorities, men of kindred character with themselves, in order that the gospel might be fully preached, and the people cared for—and Laud prevents. It is not more strange than sad, that in this nineteenth century, men should be found maintaining that Laud did right—that in entering among ' the things to be done,' the overthrow of the 'Feoffees,' or the frustration of an earnest effort whereby men of God, in the truest sense, would have 'fed the flock of God, which he hath redeemed with his own blood,' he came to a resolution, and in the execution of it performed a service, to be remembered and praised, not deplored. But, indeed, such defences only mask a deeper hatred. For often, as Lovell Beddoes puts it—

* Thoughts in the Cloister and the Crowd. 1835, 12mo, page 9.
† The History of the Troubles and Trial of Archbishop Laud. Works (edited by Scott and Bliss in ' Anglo-Catholic Library'), vol. iv. pp. 302–306.

'These are the words that grow, like grass and nettles
Out of dead men; and speckled hatreds hide,
Like toads, among them.'*

There is always a certain nimbus of glory around a decollated head, and I am disposed to concede that a truer man, great among the small, fell on Tower Hill than he whose face paled on the awful block of Whitehall window, though it was a king's and has been canonized as a martyr's. There was a stout-heartedness in the face of fearful odds in the stricken and forsaken primate throughout his trial that commands a measure of respect; and, perhaps, such is the inscrutable mystery of poor human nature, he deceived himself into a conscientious suppression of all consciences that differed from his own. Neither would I forget that one or two, or even three or four—Hall and Prideaux, Ussher, Davenant, and William Chillingworth—may be named, who, self-contradictorily, were advanced in the church more or less by him.† I will not conceal this, though historic candour compels me to affirm that, in so far as they fell in with his wishes (taking Bishop Hall as an example), they stained the white of their souls, and that Ussher and the apostolic Bedell and Chillingworth protested against the ultimate development of his views and actings.

I gladly give him all praise for his honest and courageous word to the king, when his irreverent Majesty came in too late and interrupted ' prayers.' It was a brave and worthy request that he made that the king should be present ' at prayers as well as sermon every Sunday.' ‡

I found no common joy also in coming, in the arid pages of the 'Diary,' upon these pitying words about a very venerable Puritan, gleaming like a drop of dew, or even a human tear :—' In Leicester the dean of the Arches suspended one Mr Angell, who had continued a lecturer in that great town for these divers years, without any license at all to preach, yet took liberty enough. I doubt his violence hath cracked his brain, and do therefore use him more tenderly, *because I see the hand of God hath overtaken him.*' §

Brook ('Lives of the Puritans' ‖) testily criticises the entry. The conclusion was false, for the ' violence ' of the good Angell was the ' fine frenzy ' of a man in awful earnest, in a fashion which Laud could not so much as apprehend. Still he is entitled to the full advantage of it, and to have it placed beside the kindred touch-

---

* Poems : Posthumous and Collected, vol. i. p. 109.

† ' Advanced.' The most has been made of this in the following acute and, in certain respects, valuable pamphlet :—' A Letter to the Rev. J. C. Ryle, A.B., in Reply to his Lecture on " Baxter and his Times." By a Clergyman of the Diocese of Exeter. Exeter, 1853. 8vo.'

‡ Diary, Nov. 14. 1626.   § Ap. for 1634, pp, 325–6.   ‖ Brook, iii. 286.

ing notices of his dying servants, his love for whom is remarkable.* But with every abatement, unless we are to blur the noblest names of the Christianity of England ; to write 'false' against its truest, and refuse honour to men who, rather than fail in fealty to what they believed was written in the word of God, hazarded all that was dear to them ; unless we are to overtop the loftiest intellects by one of the lowest, and sanctified genius and learning by one who was no scholar, and even could not write tolerable English, we must denounce every attempt to exalt and extol the morbid craving for an impossible 'uniformity' of this hard, cruel, unlovingly zealous, and unlovable man, around whom there hangs but a single gentle memory of tenderness to frailty or mercy to penitence ; from whose pen there never once flowed one true word for Christ or the salvation of souls ; from whom, in his darkened end, there came not so much as that remorseful touch that wins our sympathy for a Stephen Gardiner, '*Erravi cum Petro at non flevi cum Petro.*'† Claverhouse, the 'bloody,' and the first Charles, the 'false,' have been idealised. We look upon their pensive faces, and feel how traitorous they must have been to their better nature. But Laud it is not possible to idealise. The more, successive biographers have elucidated his history ; they have only the more made him a definite object of contempt. He was elevated above men who, by head and shoulders (and we know what the head includes), were taller than himself.‡ The stilts fell from beneath him, and he found his level, as 'imbecile' (it is Lord Macaulay's word), as contemptible, as worthless a man as ever rose to power—a mitred Robespierre. A certain party are voluble in pronouncing their judgments upon the victims of Laud. It were to play false to truth to let them go unanswered; and the present is undoubtedly an occasion demanding such answer and out-speaking. But—

> ' I say not that the man I praise
> By that poor tribute stands more high,
> I say not that the man I blame
> Be not of purer worth than I ;

* Laud's servants. I give one entry in Diary :—'Sept. 23. 1621.—Thy. Mr Adam Torless, my ancient, loving, and faithful servant, then my steward, after he had served me full forty-two years, died, to my great loss and grief.'

† Gardiner. Foss's Judges of England, v. 370.

‡ A few wise words from 'Thoughts in the Cloister and the Crowd' may enforce our remarks—'Perhaps it is the secret thought of many that an ardent love of power and wealth, however culpable in itself, is nevertheless a proof of superior sagacity. But in answer to this it has been well remarked, that even a child can clench its little hand the moment it is born ; and if they imagine that the successful, at any rate, must be sagacious, let them remember the saying of a philosopher, that the meanest reptiles are found at the summit of the loftiest pillars.' (Pp. 20–1.)

But when I move reluctant lips
For holy justice, human right,
The sacred cause I strive'to plead
Lends me its favour and its might.'*

CHAPTER IX.

SIBBES'S 'INTRODUCTIONS' TO WORKS OF CONTEMPORARIES.

Whitaker—Duke of York—Paul Bayne—Henry Scudder—Ezekiel Culverwell—Dr
John Preston—John Smith—John Ball—Richard Capel.

But I turn the leaf, and pass on in our 'Memoir.' And it is a
pleasant change to turn from a Laud, chaffering over the breadth
of a phylactery ; from a Mountagu, overwhelming holy men, such as
Samuel Ward, with the ribaldry of a 'Gagg for the new gospel !—
no, a new gagg for an old goose!' from a Wren, tracking every
'two or three' who sought to meet together in the name of
the Lord, to Richard Sibbes at his post, discharging his duties
as a minister of Christ through 'good and evil report,' and sus-
taining the kindliest relationship with all the 'good men and true'
of his contemporaries. There are pleasant memorials of the latter
in various occasional productions, such as 'prefaces' and 'epistles
dedicatory,' which Sibbes from time to time prefixed to good books
of good men. These I would now bring together. They give us
some very precious glimpses of his society, from a pretty early date
to near the close. They are, indeed, so many little 'essays' on religious subjects, written in his very best style, and breathing all the
sweetness, and informed with all the spirituality, of his larger writings.
Where can we turn to more felicitous words about 'faith,' and
'prayer,' and 'holiness,' and the 'Christian life'? while there is a
modesty of praise of the author introduced, whether living or dead,
in striking contrast with the adulation then prevalent. First of all,
I find among the 'Epicedia in Obitum Gul: Whitakeri,'† a copy of
Greek verses to the memory of that truly great man, whose mother
was Elizabeth Nowell, sister of Dr Alexander Nowell, and who, if he
had found such a biographer as Nowell has in Archdeacon Churton,
would be better known to the present generation. As a Master
of Sibbes's own College of St John's, and as having married a sister
first of Samuel and Ezekiel Culverwell, and next the widow of
Dudley Fenner, and in every-day association with the Culverwells

---

* 'Passion-Flowers,' by Mrs Howe. Boston, 1854, p. 113.
† Works, Geneva, fol. 1610, vol. i. p. 706; previously published in 1596. 4to.

MEMOIR OF RICHARD SIBBES, D.D.

and Fenners, Cartwright, Fuller, Chadderton, and Dod, Whitaker could not but be known and esteemed by him. He was venerated by all parties. He was, says even the atrabilious Anthony Wood, 'one of the greatest men his college ever produced, the desire and love of the present times and the envy of posterity, that cannot bring forth a parallel.'* 'The learned Whitaker,' observes Leigh, 'the honour of our schools and the angel of our church, than whom our age saw nothing more memorable.'† 'Who,' exclaims Bishop Hall, 'ever saw him without reverence, or heard him without wonder?'‡ Whitaker died in 1596, the second year of Sibbes's studentship. It is significant that the verses of such a mere youth received a place beside the tributes of the greatest men of the age :—

Τὴν ὀρθὴν πάροδον πολλοις, 'ραιστῆρα Παπιστῶν
Σαυτὸν γνωρίζεις, Οὐϊτάχηρε, σοφοις
Ἔξοχος ἁπάντων, ὃ δ᾽ἀνεδραμεν ἐρνεῖ ἴσος,
Καὶ Μουσῶν ὀρθῶς τὰς ἀνέψγε θύρας.
Εὔθετα τ᾽ἐκδίδου, 'ρ᾽ ἔμφρων καὶ πλοια κυβερνῶν
Τὴν λύμην κακὴν ζῶν τε θανών τ᾽ἔφυγε.
Νῦν γε ἀείμνηστον φήμην, κῦδος τε μέγιστον,
Λιπών, πηγάζει δόγματα θεσπέσια.

R[ICHARD] S[IBBES].§

It is hardly worth while turning these verses into English, but one remark is suggested by them. Spite of the ''ραιστῆρα Παπιστῶν' (= hammer of the papists), won by his controversies with Campian and Bellarmine and others, Bellarmine thought so highly of Whitaker that he sent for his portrait, and gave it a prominent place in his study ; and when his friends were introduced to him he used to point to it and say, 'he was the most learned heretic he ever read.'||

Though it anticipates the order in date, it may be as well to introduce here the only other verses of Sibbes that are known (this time Latin)—on the birth of the Duke of York :—¶

* Fasti Oxon. (ed. by Bliss, vol. i. p. 210, &c.)

† Edward Leigh's Treatise of Religion and Learning, folio, 1656, p. 363.

‡ Quoted in Leigh, supra, p. 364. Hall wrote an English 'Elegy' and Latin verses on Whitaker. The former will be found in Caroli Horni Carmen Funebre in Obitum Ornatissimi viri Gul., Whitakeri, &c. Lond. 4to, 1596. The latter pre-fixed to Whitaker's Prælectiones, 1599, 4to. Both, in Hall's Works by Peter Hall, xii. 323–25 and 330.   § Given verbatim et literatim from the volume of Whitaker.

|| Wood's Athenæ, ante. For full notice of Whitaker, with, as usual, ample authorities, consult Cooper's Athenæ Cantab., vol. ii., p. 196, seq.

¶ From 'Ducis Eboracensis Fasciæ a Musis Cantabrigiensibus,' 1633, p. 6. For pointing out both the Greek and Latin verses I am indebted to Charles H. Cooper, Esq., Cambridge, not more erudite than willing to place his multitudinous collections at the disposal of a fellow-labourer.

IN NATALEM DUCIS EBORACENSIS AUSPICATISSIMUM.

Anglia ter felix, ternâ jam prole beata :
    Pax regno namque est pignore firma novo.
Major si ex populi numero sit gloria regis ;
    Natorum ex numero an non magè surgit honos ?
Candidiora nitent tria Lilia, tresque Leones
    Exultant, sceptra ut nobilitata vident,
Fratribus et binis stipatur utrinque Maria :
    Delicias junctas cum Patre Mater habet.
Regia stirps crescit ; crescunt hinc gaudia regni :
    Crescat et hinc summo gloria summa Deo !

At Tu, Magne puer, Regum de stemmate germen,
    Cura Dei, Patriæ spes nova, vive, vige.
Gloria Te niveis semper circumvolet alis,
    Teque ipso major crescito, parve puer !
Gratia te et virtus semper comitentur euntem !
    In vultu et labris sessitet ipsa *Charis !*
Angelicusque chorus tua stet cunabula circum,
    Sitque *Duci* semper *Dux* DEUS atque *Comes!*
Et nati natorum, et qui nascentur ab illis
    Perpetuent seriem, *Carole* magne, tuam !
Germinet usquè, ferax jam faustè, regia vitis
    Germinet, O fructus edat et usquè novos !

R[ICHARD] S[IBBES], *Aulæ Sanctæ Catharinæ Præfectus.* *

It were a waste of pains to translate these lines. Neither their
subject nor their merit claims this.†

It is clear that Sibbes wanted the *afflatus* of the poet, of whom
the old axiom, one of the world's *memorabilia,* must ever hold,
nascitur non fit. And alas! for the '*gratia,*' and other prayers!
for this Duke of York became the Second Charles of England.

Returning upon our chronology, Paul Bayne, whose 'ministry'
along with Sibbes has been described in an earlier part of this
Memoir,‡ having died in 1617, there was issued immediately a
quarto volume containing an Exposition of the 1st chapter of the
Epistle to the Ephesians.§ Its main theme is 'Predestination,'
one of the '*doctrinal*' points forbidden by royal proclamation to
be discussed. Soberly, wisely, suggestively, and with much beauty
of wording does Sibbes introduce his 'father in the gospel.'

' Notwithstanding the world's complaint of the surfeit of books (hasty
wits being over forward to vent their unripe and misshapen conceits), yet

---

* This also is given *verbatim* from the volume.

† Perhaps the classical scholar will agree with me, that in the couplet,
    Gratia te et virtus semper comitentur euntem,
        In vultu et labris sessitet ipsa Charis !
— 'May grace itself sit on thy countenance and lips,' we have a reminiscence of a
fragment from Diodorus πειθώ τις ἐπικάθισεν ἐπι τοις χείλεσιν = 'Persuasion sat
upon his lips.' Quoted in Keightley's History of Greece, p. 160.

‡ See pages xxxvi, xxxviii.

§ Commentary on 1st Chapter of Ephesians, handling the controversy of Predestination, 4to, 1618.

in all ages there hath been, and will be necessary uses of holy treatises, appliable to the variety of occasions of the time; because men of weaker conceits cannot so easily of themselves discern how one truth is inferred from another, and proved by another, especially when truth is controverted by men of more subtile and stronger wits. Whereupon, as God's truth hath in all ages been opposed in some branches of it; so the divine providence that watcheth over the church, raised up some to fence the truth, and make up the breach. Men gifted proportionably to the time, and as well furnished to fight God's battles, as Satan's champions have been to stand for him: neither have any points of Scripture been more exactly discussed, than those that have been most sharply oppugned, opposition whetting both men's wits and industry, and in several ages men have been severally exercised. The ancientest of the fathers had to deal with them without (the Pagans), and especially with proud heretics, that made their own conceits the measure of holy truth, believing no more than they could comprehend in the articles of the Trinity, and natures of Christ, whence they bent their forces that way, and for their matter wrote more securely. Not long after, the enemies of grace, and flatterers of nature, stirred up St Augustine to challenge the doctrine of God's predestination and grace out of their hands, which he did with great success, as fitted with grace, learning, and wit for such a conflict, and no Scriptures are more faithfully handled by him, than those that were wrested by his opposites, and such as made for the strengthening of of his own cause. In other writings he took more liberty, his scholars Prosper, Fulgentius and others interest themselves in the quarrel.

In process of time, men desirous of quiet, and tired with controversies, began to lay aside the study of Scriptures, and hearken after an easier way of ending strife, by the determination of one man (the Bishop of Rome), whom virtually they made the whole church; so the people were shut up under ignorance and implicit faith, which pleased them well, as easing them of labour of search, as upon the same irksomeness of trouble in the eastern parts, they yielded to the confusion and abomination of Mahometism.

And lest scholars should have nothing to do, they were set to tie and untie school knots, and spin questions out of their own brain, in which brabbles they were so taken up, that they slightly looked to other matters; as for questions of weight they were schooled to resolve all into the decisive sentence of the see apostolic, the authority of which they bent their wits to advance; yet then wisdom found children to justify her: for Scriptures that made for authority of princes and against usurpation of popes, were well cleared by Occam, Marsilius, Patavinus, and others, as those of predestination and grace by Ariminensis, Bradwardine, and their followers, against Pelagianism, then much prevailing. At length the apostasy of popery spread so far, that God in pity to his poor church, raised up men of invincible courage, unwearied pains, and great skill in tongues and arts to free religion, so deeply enthralled; from whence it is that we have so many judicious tractates and commentaries in this latter age. And yet will there be necessary use of farther search into the Scriptures as new heresies arise, or old are revived, and further strengthened. The conviction of which, is then best when their crookedness is brought to the straight rule of Scriptures to be discovered. Besides, new expositions of Scriptures will be useful, in respect of new temptations, corruptions in life and cases of conscience, in which the mind will not receive any satisfying resolution, but from explication and application of Scriptures. Moreover, it is not unprofitable that there should be divers treatises of the same portion of Scriptures, because the same truth may be better conveyed to the conceits of some men, by some men's handling than others', one man relishing one man's gifts more than another. And it is not meet that the glory of God's goodness and wisdom should be obscured, which shineth in the variety of men's gifts, especially seeing the depth of Scripture is such, that though men had large hearts, as the sand of the sea shore, yet could they not empty out all things contained ; for though the main principles be not many, yet deductions and conclusions are infinite, and until Christ's second coming to judgment, there will never want new occasion of further search and wading into these deeps.

In all which respects this exposition of this holy man, deserves acceptance of the church, as fitted to the times (as the wise reader will well discern). Some few places are not so full as could be wished, for clearing some few obscurities ; yet those that took the care of setting them out, thought it better to let them pass as they are, than be over-bold with another man's work, in making him speak what he did not, and take them as they be. The greatest shall find matter to exercise themselves in ; the meaner, matter of sweet comfort and holy instruction, and all confess, that he hath brought some light to this excellent portion of Scripture.

He was a man fit for this task, a man of much communion with God, and acquaintance with his own heart, observing the daily passages of his life, and exercised much with spiritual conflicts. As St Paul in this epistle never seemeth to satisfy himself in advancing the glory of grace; and the vileness of man in himself, so this our Paul had large conceits of these things, a deep insight into the mystery of God's grace, and man's corruption : he could therefore enter further into Paul's meaning, having received a large measure of Paul's spirit. He was one that sought no great matters in the world, being taken up with comforts and griefs, unto which the world is a stranger ; one that had not all his learning out of books ; of a sharp wit, and clear judgment : though his meditations were of a higher strain than ordinary, yet he had a good dexterity, furthered by his love to do good, in explaining dark points with lightsome similitudes. His manner of handling questions in this epistle is press, and school-like, by arguments on both sides, conclusions, and answers, a course more suitable to this purpose than loose discourses.

In setting down the object of God's predestination, he succeeds him in opinion, whom he succeeded in place ;* in which point divines accord not who in all other points do jointly agree against the troubles of the church's peace, in our neighbour countries ; for some would have man lie before God in predestinating him, as in lapsed and miserable estate ; others would have God in that first decree to consider man abstracted from such respects, and to be considered of, as a creature alterable, and capable either of happiness or misery, and fit to be disposed of by God, who is Lord of his own to any supernatural end ; yet both agree in this : First, that there was an eternal separation of men in God's purpose. Secondly, that this first decree of severing man to his ends, is an act of sovereignty over his creature, and altogether independent of anything in the creature, as a cause of it, especially in comparative reprobation, as why he rejected Judas, and not Peter ; sin foreseen cannot be the cause, because that was common to both, and therefore could be no cause of severing. Thirdly, all agree in this, that damnation is an act of divine justice, which supposeth demerit ; and therefore the execution of God's decree is founded on sin, either of nature, or life, or both. My meaning is not to make the cause

* Perkins.

71

mine, by unnecessary intermeddling. The worthiness of the men on both side is such, that it should move men to moderation in their censures either way. Neither is this question of like consequence with others in this business, but there is a wide difference between this difference and other differences. And one cause of it, is the difficulty of understanding, how God conceives things, which differs in the whole kind from ours, he conceiving of things altogether and at once without discourse, we one thing after another, and by another. Our comfort is, that what we cannot see in the light of nature and grace, we shall see in the light of glory, in the university of heaven ; before which time, that men should in all matters have the same conceit of things of this nature, is rather to be wished for, than to be hoped. That learned bishop (now with God) that undertook the defence of Mr Perkins, hath left to the church, together with the benefit of his labours, the sorrow for his death, the fame of his worth, an example likewise of moderation, who, though he differed from Mr Perkins in this point, yet shewed that he could both assent in lesser things, and with due respect maintain in greater matters.* If we should discern of differences, the church would be troubled with fewer distempers ; I speak not as if way were to be given to Vorstian, lawless, licentious liberty of prophecy ; that every one, so soon as he is big of some new conceit, should bring forth his abortive monster : for thus the pillars of Christian faith would soon be shaken, and the church of God, which is a house of order, would become a Babel, a house of confusion. The doleful issues of which pretended liberty, we see in Polonia, Transylvania, and in countries nearer hand. We are much to bless God for the king's majesty's firmness this way, unto whose open appearing in these matters, and to the vigilancy of some in place, we owe our freedom from that schism, that troubleth our neighbours.

But for diversity of apprehensions of matters far remote from the foundation ; these may stand with public and personal peace. I will keep the reader no longer from the treatise ; the blessing of heaven go with it, that through the good done by it, much thanksgiving may be to God in the Church ! Amen.   R. SIBBS.

Gray's Inn.

Our next name is Henry Scudder, whom Richard Baxter and John Owen united to praise while he was alive. In 1620, he published his inestimable little treatise, worthy companion to his ' Christian's Daily Walk in Holy Security and Peace,' entitled ' Key of Heaven, the Lord's Prayer Opened.'† To it Sibbes prefixed a ' Recom-

---

* The 'learned bishop' is Robert Abbot, Bishop of Salisbury, and the reference is to his ' Defence of the Reformed Catholick of W. Perkins against Dr W. Bishop.' 4to, 1611.

† A Key of Heaven : the Lord's Prayer opened, and so applied, that a Christian may learn how to pray, and to procure all things which may make for the glory of God, and the good of himself, and of his neighbour. Containing likewise such doctrines of faith and goodness, as may be very useful to all that desire to live godly in Christ Jesus. The second edition, enlarged by the author. Mat. vii. 7, Ask, and it shall be given you ; seek, and ye shall find ; knock, and it shall be opened unto you. *Oratio justi clavis cœli.* London : Printed by Thomas Harper, for Benjamin Fisher, and are to be sold at the sign of the Talbot in Aldersgate Street. 1633. This ' Key ' has been erroneously included among Sibbes's own writings, *e. g.*, Brook (' Lives of Puritans, ii. 420), and even in Dr Bliss's Sale-Catalogue.

mendation,' which is in itself an Essay on Prayer, of rare value. Scudder was a contemporary of Sibbes in Cambridge, of Christ's Church. Afterwards he became successively minister at Drayton, in Oxfordshire, and at Collingborn-Dukes, in Wiltshire. In the year 1643, he was chosen one of the 'Assembly of Divines,' and was exemplary in his attendance. His books are pre-eminently scriptural and practical, and there are occasional similes and scraps of out-of-the-way incidents of a quaint beauty and appositeness. It is easy to understand that such a man would be dear to Richard Sibbes.* Thus he writes :—

To be much in persuading those that be favourites of some great person, to use that interest for their best advantage, were an endeavour somewhat needless, considering natural self-love inclineth men in such cases to be sensible enough of their own good. Yet so dull is our apprehension of matters that are of an higher nature, that though we have the ear of God always open unto us, and free access to the throne of grace through Christ who appeareth in heaven for us, carrying our names in his breast, yet we need stirring up to improve this blessed liberty, though the whole world be not worth this one prerogative, that we can boldly call God Father. This disproportion of our carriage ariseth in part from Satan's malice, who laboureth to keep us in darkness, that we believe not, or mind not our best privileges, which if we did, how glorious would our lives appear! how comfortably and fruitfully should we walk! what honour should God have by us! what sweet sacrifice from us! how should we overlook all opposite power! But now by reason we are prone to believe Satan, and the lies of our own heart; and ready to call truth itself into question, as if these things were too good to be true, no marvel if we pass our days so deadly. For what use of an hidden and locked up treasure, if we use not this key of prayer to fetch from thence for all our need ? What benefit of all the precious promises made in Christ unto us, unless we allege them unto God, and with a reverend boldness bind him with his own word, which he can no more deny, than cease to be God ? If we took these things to heart, God should hear oftener from us, we would be more in heaven than we are, seeing we should bring as much grace and comfort from God as we could bring faith to grasp and carry away.

Besides this fore-mentioned mindlessness of our privileges, since the fall the soul naturally loveth to spend and scatter itself about these present sensible things, and cannot without some strife gather itself together, and fix upon heavenly things. Now this talking with God requireth an actual bent of the mind, and carrieth up the whole soul into heaven, and exerciseth, as all the parts, so all the graces of the soul, faith especially, prayer being nothing else but the flame of faith. And Satan knowing that when we send up our desires to God, it is to fetch supply against him, troubleth the soul, weak of itself, with a world of distractions. Where he cannot corrupt the doctrine of prayer (as in popery) with heresies and superstitious follies, there he laboureth to hinder the exercise of it. Wherein we should be so far from being discouraged, that we should reason rather that must needs be an excellent duty which is so irksome to the flesh, and which the devil so eagerly sets against. This should encourage us to this exercise, wherein

* Scudder. Consult Brook's ' Lives of the Puritans,' ii. 504, *seq.*

lieth all our strength, that if in spite of Satan's annoyance and our own indisposition, we will set upon this duty, we shall find ourselves by little and little more raised up to heaven, and our hearts more and more enlarged, God rewarding the use of that little grace we find at the first, with increase of strength and comfort. To him that hath (in the exercise of that he hath) shall be given more. We should labour not to be ignorant of Satan's enterprises, who besides his diverting our minds from prayer, and disturbing us in it, laboureth by all means to draw us to some sin, the conscience whereof will stop our mouths, and stifle our prayers, and shake our confidence, and eclipse our comfort; which he oft aimeth more at than the sin itself unto which he tempteth us. We should labour therefore to preserve ourselves in such a state of soul, wherein we might have boldness with God, and wherein this gainful trading with him might not be hindered.

To pass over many other causes of the neglect of this intercourse, and dealing with God by prayer, we may well judge, as one of the chief, a self-sufficiency whereby men dwell too much in themselves. He that hath nothing at home will seek abroad. The poor man (saith Solomon) speaketh supplications. If we were poor in spirit, and saw our own emptiness, it would force us out of ourselves. Alas! what temptation can we resist, much less overcome, without fresh succour? What cross can we endure without impatience, if we have not new support? What success can we look for, yea, in common affairs, without his blessing? What good can we do, nay, think of, without new strength? When we do any good by his power, do we not need pardon for the blemishes of our best performances? What good blessing can we enjoy, so as we defile not ourselves in it, without a further blessing, giving us with the thing the holy use of it? Yet we see most men content to receive blessings as they come from God's general providence, without regarding any sanctified use by prayer, whereas holy men, knowing that God will be sought unto even for those things of which he hath given a promise, Ezek. xxxvi. 37, in obedience to this his divine order, desire to receive all from him as a fruit of their prayers. And God's manner is to keep many blessings from his children until they have begged them, as delighting to hear his children speak. The consideration whereof moveth those that have nearest communion with God to acknowledge him in all their ways, depending on him for direction, strength, success, whereupon he delighteth in shewing himself more familiarly unto them in the sweetest experiences of his love, guiding them by his counsel whilst they abide here, and after, bringing them to glory, Ps. xxxvii. 24. As other graces grow in those that are in the state of grace, so this spirit of prayer receiveth continual increase upon more inward acquaintance with God, and their own estates. Whence they can never be miserable, having God to pour forth their spirits and ease their hearts unto, who cannot but regard the voice of his own Spirit in them. But of ourselves, such is our case, that God who knoweth us better than we know ourselves, saith, we know not what or how to pray, Rom. viii. 26. This language of Canaan is strange unto us. Which our blessed Saviour in mercy considering, stirred up a desire in his disciples to be taught of him the Son, how to speak to the Father. Where thereupon he teacheth them a form, which for heavenly fulness of matter, and exactness of order, sheweth that it could come from no other Author.

This holy pattern comprising so much in so little, all things to be desired in six short petitions, it is needful for the guides of God's people to lay open the riches of it to the view of those that are less exercised. An endeavour which his excellent majesty thought not unbeseeming the greatness of a king. For the use of a set form of prayer, and this in special, I will make no question; yet in the use of this prayer, we may dwell more in the meditation and enforcing such petitions as shall concern our present occasions. For instance, if ever there were time of praying, 'Let thy kingdom come,' let Christ arise and his enemies be scattered, then certainly now is the time for us to ascend up into heaven by our prayers, and awake Christ, that he would rebuke the winds and waves, and cause a calm; that he would be strong for his church, in maintaining his own cause. It is God's manner, before any great work for his church, to stir up the spirits of his beloved ones to give him no rest. How earnest was Daniel with the Lord immediately before the delivery out of Babylon, Dan. xi. And undoubtedly, if we join the forces of our prayers together, and set upon God with an holy violence, he would set his power, his wisdom, his goodness on work for the exalting of his church, and ruin of the enemies of it. Now is the time for Moses his hands to be upheld, whilst Amalek goeth down.

The prevailing power of prayer with God in times of danger, appeareth not only in the sacred history of the Bible, but hath been recorded in all ages of the church. In the primitive church, A.D. 175, the army of Christians was called the thundering legion, because, upon their prayers, God scattered their enemies with thunder, and refreshed themselves with showers in a great drought.

After, in the good Emperor Theodosius his time, A.D. 394, upon an earnest prayer to Christ, the winds fought from heaven for him against his enemies, as they did for us in 1588. And continually since, God never left the force of faithful prayer without witness. If we would observe how God answereth prayers, we should see a blessed issue of all the holy desires he kindles in our hearts; for he cannot but make good that title whereby he is styled, 'a God hearing prayer,' Ps. lxv. 2, which should move us to sow more prayers into his bosom, the fruit whereof we should reap in our greatest need. It would be a strong evidence in these troublesome times of the future good success of the church, if we were earnest in soliciting Christ with these words which himself hath taught us, 'Let thy kingdom come.' For put him to it, and 'he will never fail those that seek him,' Ps. ix. 10. He loveth importunity.

But to speak something of this treatise of this godly and painful minister of Christ, which is written by him without affectation, as desirous to clothe spiritual things with a spiritual manner of writing, the diligent and godly reader shall observe a sound, clear, substantial handling of the greatest points that naturally fall within the discourse, and a more large and useful unfolding of many things, than in former treatises. It appeareth he sought the good of all; so that, besides the labours of other holy men, there will be just cause of blessing God for his assistance in this work. To whose blessing I commend both it and the whole Israel of God.

Gray's Inn.   R. SIBBES.

Passing on to 1623–4, we have a delightful 'epistle' prefixed to Ezekiel Culverwell's 'Treatise of Faith . . . . . applied especially unto the use of the weakest Christians.' * This little volume had

---

* A Treatise of Faith. Wherein is declared how a man may live by faith, and find relief in all his necessities. Applied especially unto the use of the weakest Christians. By Ezekiel Culverwell. The just shall live by faith. The seventh

passed through seven editions by 1633 ; and it were well if its popularity could be revived ; for it overflows with profound thought, sagacious counsel, pungent appeal, and true eloquence. But let Dr Gouge characterise it and its author. ' God,' he says, ' sent Ezekiel Culverwell, as of old he sent Ezekiel Buzi, to set forth the promises of God more plentifully and pertinently than ever before ; and that to breed faith where it is not, to strengthen it where it is weak, to settle it where it wavereth, to repair it where it decayeth, to apply it aright to every need, to extend it to sanctification as well as to justification, and to point out the singular use of it in matters temporal, spiritual, and eternal.' And he adds—' What I say of him, I know of him ; for from mine infancy have I known him, and under his ministry was I trained up in my younger years, he being at least two-and-twenty years older than myself.' *

Let us now read Sibbes's ' Epistle to the Christian Reader :'—

The leading of a happy life (the attainment whereof this treatise directeth unto) is that which all desire, but God's truth only discovereth, and faith only enjoyeth. In the first Adam, our happiness was in our own keeping ; but he, by turning from God to the creature, made proof what and whence he was ; a creature raised out of nothing, and without the supporting power of him in whom all things consist, subject to fall into a state worse than nothing again. Hence God, out of his infinite power, and depth of goodness intending the glory of his mercy, in restoring man, would not trust man with his own happiness ; but would have it procured and established in the person of a second Adam, in whom we recover a surer estate than we lost in the first. For though Adam's soul was joined to God, yet that knitting was within the contingent and changeable liberty of his own will ; but now we are brought to God in an everlasting covenant of mercy, by faith in Christ ; who, by taking the nature of man into unity of his person, and not the person of any, became a public person, to be the author of eternal salvation to all that receive him ; and so gathering us that were scattered from God, into one head, bringeth us back again to God, by a contrary way to that whereby we fell, that is, by cleaving to God by faith, from whom we fell by distrust. A fit grace for the state of grace, giving the whole glory to God, and emptying the soul of all self-sufficiency, and enlarging it to receive what is freely wrought and offered by another. Thus we come to have the comfort, and God the glory of mercy ; which sweet attribute moved him to set all other attributes on work to make us happy. Out of the bowels of which mercy, as he chose us to eternal salvation in Christ, so vouchsafeth he all things necessary to life and godliness. And as the same love in God giveth us heaven, and furnisheth us with all things needful in the way, until we come thither ; so the same faith which saveth us, layeth hold likewise on the promises of necessary assistance, comfort, provision, and protection : and

edition, corrected and amended. Ephes. vi. 16, ' Above all, taking the shield of faith.' Rom. xv. 4, ' Whatsoever things were written aforetime, were written for our learning, that we through patience and comfort of the Scriptures might have hope.' London : Printed by J. D. for Hen. Overton, and are to be sold at his shop at the entering in of Pope's-head Alley, out of Lumbard Street, 1633.

* ' To the Christian Reader,' prefixed to Treatise of Faith, *supra.*

this office it performeth in all the several stations of this life, until it hath brought us unto the enjoying of him ' in whose presence is fulness of joy for evermore,' Ps. xvi. 11.

We see that same love in parents, which moveth them to give an inheritance to their sons, moveth them likewise to provide for them, and to train them up in experience of their fatherly care. So it pleaseth our first and best Father, besides the main promise of salvation, to give us many other rich and precious promises, that in taste of his goodness and truth in these, we may at length yield up our souls to him, as to our faithful Creator, 1 Pet. iv. 19, with the more assured comfort; and the longer we live here, be more rooted in faith. ' I know whom I have trusted,' 2 Tim. i. 12, saith aged St Paul. But alas! how little is that we know of his ways, Job xxvi. 14, because we observe him not, making good his word unto us! ' All his ways are mercy and truth,' Ps. xxv. 10, and every ' word is a tried word,' Ps. xii. 6. For the better help of God's people, to know their portion in those good things, which their father not only layeth up for them, Ps. xxxi. 19, for times to come, but layeth out for them here as his wisdom seeth fit ; this reverend and holy man of God hath compiled this treatise, wherein he layeth open the veins of promises hidden in the Scriptures, to the view of every Christian, and digesteth them in their orders ; and withal, sheweth their several value and use, for the beautifying of a holy life ; which wits less exercised, of themselves, would not so well have discerned.

Now that we may the rather benefit ourselves by this treatise, it will not be inconvenient to know these four things.

First, that it supposeth a reader grounded in the knowledge of the nature and properties of God, of Christ and his offices, of the covenant of grace, and such like : because as in an arch, one stone settleth another, so there is such a linking together of points in divinity, that one strengtheneth another. For from whence hath faith that efficacy, but because it is that which is required in the covenant, to lay hold on the free promises ? And whence have the promises their strength, but from the constant nature of Jehovah ; who giveth a being to his word, and is at peace with us, by the all-sufficient sacrifice of the Mediator of the new covenant? Words have their validity from the authority of the speaker. Were not faith founded on the word of an infinite God, so thoroughly appeased, the soul would sink in great temptations, whereas now even mountains vanish before a believing soul. For what can stand against Christ, who is able to subdue all to himself? Hence it is, that now we are by faith, Phil. iii. 21, safer than Adam in Paradise, because we have a promise, which he wanted. Safer it is to be as low as hell with a promise, than in paradise without it, because faith wrought by the power of God, hath what strength God hath, on whom it resteth, and therefore worketh such wonders : God honouring that grace, which honours him so much.

But howsoever the knowledge of these things serveth the argument in hand ; yet it must not be expected, that he should be long in these things, which are but coincident, and should be foreknown : which I speak, because some of weaker judgment, not considering the just bounds of treatises, may expect larger handling of some things. Whereas he hath laboured especially to furnish the argument in hand, and not to load the discourse.

In the second place, it must be known, that the fruit of these things belong to such as are in Christ, in whom all promises are yea and amen, made and performed. He that by the immortal seed of the word and Spirit is born again, may claim a title to that he is born unto. These promises be as well his inheritance, as heaven itself is. For clearing of this, there be three degrees of promises ; one of salvation to absolute and personal obedience ; but this, by reason of weakness of the flesh, driveth us to a despair of ourselves, and so to the second promise of life by Christ. This requireth nothing but receiving by faith, which is wrought in those that are given to Christ, whilst grace is offered, the Spirit clothing the words with a hidden and strong power, and making them operative ; when they are commanded to believe, their hearts are opened to believe. To persons in this estate, are made a third kind of promises, of all that is needful in this world, until all promises end in performance. Of both these promises, and the last especially, this book speaketh.

Thirdly, it must be pressed upon those that mean to profit, that they resolve to come under Christ's government, and be willing to be led by the Spirit into all revealed truth. Wisdom is easy to such as are willing ; and the victory is as good as gotten, when the will is brought from thraldom to base affections, to resolve to be guided. For such a heart lieth open to God's gracious working, and the Spirit readily closeth with such a spirit, as putteth not bars of obstinacy.

Notwithstanding, we must know in the fourth place, that when we are at the best, we shall yet be in such a conflicting state, as that we shall long after that glorious liberty of the sons of God, after we have done the work God hath given us to do. For God will have a difference betwixt heaven and earth ; and sharpen our desire of the coming of his kingdom, which nothing doth so much, especially in times of outward prosperity, as those tedious combats of the inner man. And yet let this raise up our spirits, that it is so far that this remainder should prejudice our interest in happiness, that thereby we are driven every day to renew our claim to the promise of pardon, and so to live by faith until this unclean issue be dried up. These sour herbs help us to relish Christ the better. Moreover, though in this life our endeavours come short of our desires, and we always allow a greater measure than we can attain unto ; yet we may, by stirring up the graces begun in us, and by suing God upon those promises of his Spirit and grace, whereby he hath made himself a debtor unto us, come to that measure, whereby we shall make the profession of religion glorious, and lovely in the eyes of others, and comfortable to ourselves ; and so shine far brighter than others do. Why then do we not, in the use of all sancti-fied means, beg of God, to make good the promises wherein he hath caused us to trust ? Do we not, beside life of our bodies, desire health and strength to discharge all the offices of civil life ? And why should we not much more (if the life of God be in us) labour after health and vigour of Spirit, and for that anointing of the Holy Ghost, whereby we may do and suffer all things, so as we may draw others to a liking of our ways ? The truth is, Satan laboureth to keep us under belief of particular promises, and from renewing our covenant, in confidence, that God will perfect the work that he hath begun, and not repent him of his earnest. So far as thus we cherish distrust, we lie open to Satan. Strengthen faith, and strengthen all. Let us therefore at once set upon all duties required, and be in love with an holy life, above all other lives, and put ourselves upon God's mercy and truth ; and we shall be able from experience, so far to justify all God's ways as that we would not be in another state for all the world. What greater encouragement can we wish, than that our corruptions shall fall more and more before the Spirit, and we shall be able to do all things through Christ that strengtheneth us ?

To make these ways of God more plain unto us, this pains is taken by this man of God. Not to disparage the labours of other holy men (as far as I can judge), there is nothing in this kind more fully, judiciously, or savourily written, with greater evidence of a spirit persuaded of the goodness and truth of what it sets down. And though (distinct from respect to the author) the treatise deserveth much respect, yet it should gain the more acceptance, especially of those that are babes and young men in Christ, that it is written by a father of long and reverend esteem in the church ; who hath begun in all these rules to others. As for our bodies, so for our souls, we may more securely rely on an old experienced physician. He commendeth it unto thee, having felt the kindly working of it upon himself. The Lord by his Spirit convey these truths into thy heart, and upon good felt hereby in thy soul, remember to desire God that he may still bring forth more fruit in his age, until he hath finished his course with credit to the gospel, and an assured hope of a blessed change.

Gray's Inn.   RICHARD SIBBES.

We place along with this another 'epistle' by Sibbes, prefixed to another small book by Culverwell. The copy of this in my library, was formerly in the possession of Charles I., and has his royal arms enstamped in gold on each side. Judging from its appearance, it must have been well read. The book is entitled, 'Time Well Spent in Sacred Meditations, Divine Observations, Heavenly Exhortations ;' and the 'Epistle Dedicatory' is addressed to an 'excellent Christian woman,' who seems to have been greatly beloved by Sibbes, Mrs More.* It runs as follows :—

To the right worshipful and truly religious Mrs MORE.

RIGHT WORSHIPFUL AND WORTHY MRS MORE.—The church of God hath not only benefit by exact and just treatises knit together in a methodical dependency of one part from another, but likewise of sententious independent speeches, that have a general lustre of themselves, as so many flowers in a garden, or jewels in a casket, whereof every one hath a distinct worth of themselves ; and this maketh them the more acceptable, that being short they are fitter for the heart to carry, as having much in a little.

This moved this reverend man of God, to spend what spare hours his sickness would afford him about thoughts in this kind. He was many years God's prisoner under the gout and stone, such diseases as will allow but little liberty to those that are arrested and tortured by them. So fruitful an expense of time in so weak and worn a body is seldom seen, scarce any came to him but went away better than they came ; God gave much strength of spirit to uphold his spirit from sinking under the strength of such diseases. It were a happy thing if we that are ministers of Christ, would on all conditions and times think of our calling, that our office is not tied to one day in a week, and one hour or two in that day, but that upon all fit occasions we are to quicken ourselves and others in the way homeward, as guides to heaven. We read not of the opening of heaven but to some great purpose. So it should be with the man of God, he should not open his mouth and let any thing fall (so far as frailty and the necessary occurrences of human life will permit) but what might minister some grace to the hearers.

The reason why I made choice of you to dedicate them unto, is not that

* Mrs More. She is named in his Will

79

I might discharge mine own debt unto you with another man's coin, but that I could not think of any fitter than yourself, whom this ancient minister of Christ esteemed always very much for eminency of parts and grace, and you him as a man faithful, and one that maintained his ministerial authority with good success in his place ; God allotting your habitation in your younger years in that part of the country where he lived, and where you first learned to know God and yourself. In those times those parts were in regard of the air unhealthful, yet that air was so sweetened with the savoury breath of the gospel, that they were termed the holy land. Hereupon I thought meet to commend these sententious speeches by your name to others. Which though (divers of them) may seem plain, yet what they want in show they have in weight, as coming from a man very well experienced in all the ways of God. The Lord follow you with his best blessings, that you may continue still to adorn the gospel of Christ in your place !

Yours in all Christian service,   R. Sibbes.

Before passing on to other 'Epistles' of a public kind, I would here introduce a letter to Ussher, of probably 1628–29, which happens to have been preserved. It reveals to us the keen zest and interest with which Sibbes observed what was transpiring, 'Petition of Right,' and the like. It falls in here fittingly as an introduction to the next 'Epistle,' as there is in it a passing notice of the last illness of the 'Master' of 'Emmanuel.'

Mr R. Sibbes to the Archbishop of Armagh.

Right Reverend,—My duty and service premised. I am forced of the sudden in midst of straits and distractions to write unto you, your servant being presently to depart here : but I choose rather thus to express my remembrance of your grace, than to let slip so fit an opportunity. I hope I shall always carry you in my heart, and preserve that deserved respect I owe to you, who are oft presented to me as one that God hath shewed himself unto in more than ordinary measure, and set up high in the affections of the best. I know not the man living more beholden to God, in those respects, than yourself. It went for current here a while that you were dead, which caused the hearts of many to be more refreshed upon hearing the contrary. It is very ill losing of men of much meaner service in the church in these almost desperate times. Yesterday there was an agreement between the two houses about a petition of right, whereby the liberty of the subject is like to be established. Here is much joy for it, if it prove not a lightning before death. Our fears are more than our hopes yet. Doctor Preston is inclining to a consumption, and his state is thought doubtful to the physicians. The neighbour schism getteth still more strength with us. . Boni deficiunt, mali perficiunt. I cannot now enlarge myself, your servant hastening hence. The Lord still delight to shew himself strong with you, and to shield you in the midst of all dangers, and glorify himself by you, to the great comfort of his church, and the disheartening of his enemies ! I desire your grace to remember my respect to your wife, humbly thanking you both for your undeserved love.—Your Grace's in all Christian service, to be commanded,   R. Sibbes.*

May 27.

* Ussher, ante xvi. letter ccccxxii.

We have a series of prefaces, in union with John Davenport, to various posthumous works of Dr John Preston, of whom I have had occasion to speak repeatedly in this memoir. I trust that the time is not distant when we shall have a worthy edition of his writings to place beside those of Sibbes. No books had such a wide, nay, universal audience through many generations. Edition followed upon edition, and now it is not easy to collect them all. It is mournful to think how Cambridge neglects her most illustrious sons!

The Preston epistles call for no comment beyond an explanatory word. I give them in order :—

I. The ' New Covenant or Saint's Portion.' *

Dedication.

Illustrissimis, et Honoratissimis Viris, Theophilo Comiti Lincolniensi, et Gulielmo Vice-Comiti Say et Sele, Dominis suis submississimè colendis has Johannis Prestoni, S.S. Theol. Doct., et Collegii Immanuelis Magistri Primitias Devotissimi, Tam Authoris, Dum Viveret, Quam Ipsorum, Qui Supersunt, Obsequii Testimonium, L.M.D.D.D.

RICHARDUS SIBS.
JOHANNES DAVENPORT.

To the Reader.

It had been much to have been desired (if it had so pleased the Father of spirits), that this worthy man had survived the publishing of these and other his lectures ; for then, no doubt, they would have come forth more refined and digested ; for, though there was very little or no mistake in taking them from his mouth, yet preaching and writing have their several graces. Things livened by the expression of the speaker, sometimes take well, which after, upon a mature review, seem either superfluous or flat. And we oft see men very able to render their conceits in writing, yet not the happiest speakers.

Yet we, considering (not so much what might have been, as) what now may be for the service of the church, thought good rather to communicate them thus, than that they should die with the author. He was a man of an exact judgment and quick apprehension, an acute reasoner, active in good, choice in his notions ; one who made it his chief aim to promote the cause of Christ and the good of the church, which moved him to single out arguments answerable, on which he spent his best thoughts. He was honoured of God to be an instrument of much good, whereunto he had advantage by those eminent places he was called unto. As he had a short

* The New Covenant, or the Saint's Portion: a Treatise unfolding the All-Sufficiency of God, Man's Uprightness, and the Covenant of Grace. Delivered in fourteen sermons upon Gen. xvii. 1, 2; whereunto are adjoined four sermons upon Eccles. ix. 1, 2, 11, 12. By the late faithful and worthy minister of Jesus Christ, John Preston, Dr in Divinity, Chaplain in Ordinary to his Majesty, Master of Emmanuel College in Cambridge, and sometimes preacher of Lincoln's Inn. The fourth edition, corrected. ' He hath given a portion to them that fear him : he will ever be mindful of his covenant,' Ps. cxi. 5. London : Printed by I. D. for Nicholas Bourne, and are to be sold at the south entrance of the Royal Exchange. 1630, 4to.

race to run, so he made speed, and did much in a little time. Though he was of an higher elevation and strain of spirit than ordinary, yet, out of love to do good, he could frame his conceits so as might suit with ordinary understandings. A little before his death (as we were informed by the Right Honourable the Lord Viscount Say and Sele, in whose piety, wisdom, and fidelity he put great repose), he was desirous that we should peruse what of his was fit for public use.

We are not ignorant that it is a thing subject to censure to seem bold and witty in another man's work, and, therefore, as little is altered as may be. And we desire the reader rather to take in good part that which is intended for public good, than to catch at imperfections, considering they were but taken as they fell from him speaking. And we entreat those that have anything of his in their hands, that they would not be hasty, for private respects, to publish them, till we, whom the author put in trust, have perused them. We purpose (by God's help) that what shall be judged fit shall come forth. We send forth these sermons of God's All-Sufficiency, and Man's Uprightness, and the Covenant of Grace first, as being first prepared by him that had the copies, and because the right understanding of these points hath a chief influence into a Christian life. The Lord give a blessing answerable, and continue still to send forth such faithful labourers into his harvest!

RICHARD SIBS.
JOHN DAVENPORT.

II. The 'Breastplate of Faith and Love.'*

Dedication.

Illustrissimo, Nobilissimoque Viro, Roberto Comiti Warwicensi, Johannis Prestoni, S.T.D., et Collegii Immanuelis Q.† Magistri (cujus tutelæ, dum in vivis esset, Primogenitum suum in Disciplinam et Literis expoliendum tradidit), posthumorum tractatuum partem de natura fidei, ejusque efficacia, deque amore et operibus bonis, Devotissimi, tam authoris, dum viveret, quam ipsorum qui supersunt, obsequii testimonium. M.D.D.D.

RICHARDUS SIBS.
JOHANNES DAVENPORT.

To the Christian Reader.

CHRISTIAN READER—Innumerable are the sleights of Satan, to hinder a Christian in his course towards heaven, by exciting the corruption of his own heart to disturb him, when he is about to do any good; or by discouraging him with inward terrors, when he would solace himself with heavenly comforts; or by disheartening him under the fears of sufferings,

---

* The Breastplate of Faith and Love. A treatise, wherein the ground and exercise of faith and love, as they are set upon Christ their object, and as they are expressed in good works, is explained. Delivered in 18 sermons upon three several texts, by the late faithful and worthy minister of Jesus Christ, John Preston, Dr in Divinity, chaplain in ordinary to his Majesty, Master of Emmanuel College in Cambridge, and sometimes Preacher of Lincoln's Inn. The fourth edition. 'But let us who are of the day be sober, putting on the breastplate of faith and love,' 1 Thess. v. 8. 'What will it profit, my brethren, if a man say he have faith, and hath not works? Can faith save him?' James ii. 14. Imprinted at London by R. Y. for Nicholas Bourne and are to be sold at the south entrance of the Royal Exchange. 1634.

† Qu. 'quondam?'—ED.

when he should be resolute in a good cause. A type whereof were the Israelites, whose servitude was redoubled when they turned themselves to forsake Egypt. Wherefore we have much need of Christian fortitude, according to that direction, 'Watch ye, stand fast, quit yourselves like men,' 1 Cor. xvi. 13; especially since Satan, like a serpentine crocodile pursued, is by resistance put to flight.

But as in wars (which the Philistines knew well in putting their hope in Goliath) the chief strength of the soldiers lieth in their captain, so in spiritual conflicts all a Christian's strength is in Christ, and from him. For before our conversion we were of no strength; since our conversion we are not sufficient of ourselves to think a good thought. And to work out from the saints all self-confidence, God, by their falls, teacheth them 'to rejoice in the Lord Jesus, and to have no confidence in the flesh.'

Whatsoever Christ hath for us, is made ours by faith, which is the hand of the soul enriching it by receiving Christ, who is the treasure hid in the field, and with him, those unsearchable riches of grace, which are revealed and offered in the gospel; yea, it is part of our spiritual armour. That which was fabulously spoken of the race of giants is truly said of a Christian, he is born with his armour upon him; as soon as he is regenerate he is armed. It is called a breastplate, Θώραξ, 1 Thess. v. 8, because it preserves the heart; a long, large shield, Θυρεὸς of θύρα, Eph. vi. 16 (as the word signifieth), which is useful to defend the whole man from all sorts of assaults. Which part of spiritual armour, and how it is to be managed, is declared in the former part of the ensuing treatise, in ten sermons.

Now, as all rivers return into the sea whence they came, so the believing soul, having received all from Christ, returneth all to Christ. For thus the believer reasoneth, Was God's undeserved, unexpected love such to me that he spared not his only-begotten Son, but gave him to die for me? It is but equal that I should live to him, die for him, bring in my strength, time, gifts, liberty, all that I have, all that I am, in his service, to his glory. That affection, whence these resolutions arise, is called love, which so inclineth the soul that it moveth in a direct line towards that object wherein it expecteth contentment. The soul is miserably deluded in pursuing the wind, and is taking aim at a flying fowl, whilst it seeks happiness in any creature; which appears in the restlessness of those irregular agitations and endless motions of minds of ambitious, voluptuous, and covetous persons, whose frame of spirit is like the lower part of the elementary region, the seat of winds, tempests, and earthquakes, full of unquietness; whilst the believer's soul, like that part towards heaven which is always peaceable and still, enjoyeth true rest and joy. And indeed the perfection of our spirits cannot be but in union with the chief of spirits, which communicateth his goodness to the creature according to its capacity. This affection of love, as it reflecteth upon Christ, being a fruit and effect of his love to us apprehended by faith, is the subject of the second part of the following treatise, in seven sermons.

The judicious author, out of a piercing insight into the methods of the tempter, knowing upon what rocks the faith of many suffers shipwreck; that neither the weak Christian might lose the comfort of his faith through want of evidences, nor the presumptuous rest upon a fancy instead of faith, nor the adversaries be emboldened to cast upon us, by reason of this doctrine of justification by faith only, their wonted nicknames of Solifidians and Nullifidians; throughout the whole treatise, and more especially in the last sermon, he discourseth of good works as they arise from faith and love. This is the sum of the faithful and fruitful labours of this reverend, learned, and godly minister of the gospel, who, whilst he lived, was an example of the life of faith and love, and of good works, to so many as were acquainted with his equal and even walking in the ways of God, in the several turnings and occasions of his life. But it will be too much injury to the godly reader to be detained longer in the porch. We now dismiss thee to the reading of this profitable work, beseeching God to increase faith, and to perfect love in thy heart, that thou mayest be fruitful in good works.

Thine in our Lord Jesus Christ,   RICHARD SIBBS.
JOHN DAVENPORT.

III. The Saint's Daily Exercise. *

To the Reader.

COURTEOUS READER,—To discourse largely of the necessity and use of this piece of spiritual armour, after so many learned and useful treatises upon this subject, may seem superfluous, especially considering that there is much spoken to this purpose, for thy satisfaction, in the ensuing treatise, wherein, besides the unfolding of the nature of this duty (which is the saint's daily exercise), and strong enforcement to it, there is an endeavour to give satisfaction in the most incident cases, want of clearing whereof is usually an hindrance to the cheerful and ready performance thereof. In all which, what hath been done by this reverend and worthy man we had rather should appear in the treatise itself, to thy indifferent judgment, than to be much in setting down our own opinion. This we doubt not of, that, by reason of the spiritual and convincing manner of handling this argument, it will win acceptance with many, especially considering that it is of that nature wherein, though much have been spoken, yet much more may be said with good relish to those that have any spiritual sense ; for it is the most spiritual action, wherein we have nearer communion with God, than in any other holy performance, and whereby it pleaseth God to convey all good to us, to the performance whereof Christians find most backwardness and indisposedness, and from thence most dejection of spirit, which also in these times is most necessary, wherein, unless we fetch help from heaven this way, we see the church and cause of God like to be trampled under feet. Only remember, that we let these sermons pass forth as they were delivered by himself in public, without taking that liberty of adding or detracting, which perhaps some would have thought meet ; for we thought it best that his own meaning should be expressed in his own words and manner, especially considering there is little which perhaps may seem superfluous to some, but may, by God's blessing, be useful to others. It would be a good prevention of many inconveniences in this kind, if able men would be persuaded to publish their own works in their lifetime ; yet we think it a good service to the church when that defect is supplied by giving

* The Saint's Daily Exercise ; a Treatise unfolding the whole Duty of Prayer. Delivered in five sermons upon 1 Thes. v. 17. By the late faithful and worthy minister of Jesus Christ, John Preston, Dr in Divinity, Chaplain in Ordinary to his Majesty, Master of Emmanuel College in Cambridge, and sometime Preacher of Lincoln's Inn. The fourth edition, corrected. ' The effectual fervent prayer of a righteous man availeth much,' James v. 16. ' If I regard iniquity in my heart, the Lord will not hear my prayer,' Ps. lxvi. 18. London : Printed by W. I. for Nicholas Bourne, and are to be sold at the south entrance of the Royal Exchange. 1630. 4to.

some life to those things, which otherwise would have died of themselves. The blessing of these labours of his we commend unto God, and the benefit of them unto thee, resting thine in our Lord Jesus Christ,

RICHARD SIBS.
JOHN DAVENPORT.

IV. The Saints' Qualification. *

Dedication.

Illustrissimo, Nobilissimo Viro, Philippo, Pembrochiæ, et Montis Gomerici Comiti, Baroni Herbert•de Cardiffe et Sherland, Ordinis Garterii Equiti, Regiæ Domus Camerario, Regiæ Majestati a Secretioribus Consiliis, &c., triplicem hunc Johannis Prestoni, S.S., Theologiæ Doct. Colleg. Immanuelis Nuper Magist. et Regiæ Majest. a Sacris, Tractatum, de Humiliatione, Nova Creatura, Præparatione ad Sacram Synaxin, in Devotissimæ, Tam authoris, quam Ipsorum, Observantiæ Testimonium, L.M.D.D.D.

RICHARDUS SIBS.
JOANNES DAVENPORT.

To the Christian Reader.

The good acceptance the sermons of this worthy man have found amongst well-disposed Christians, hath made us the willinger to give way to the publishing of these, as coming from the same author. The good they may thus do prevails more for the sending of them forth than some imperfections (that usually accompany the taking of other men's speeches) may do to suppress them. Something may well be yielded to public good in things not altogether so as we wish. They are enforced upon none that shall except against them, they may either read or refuse them at their pleasure. The argument of them is such as may draw the more regard, being of matters of necessary and perpetual use.

For 'Humiliation' we never so deeply see into the grounds of it (sinfulness of nature and life); or, so far as we see, look upon it with that eye of detestation we should; and therefore a holy heart desireth still further light to be brought in, to discover whatsoever may hinder communion with God, and is glad when sin is made loathsome unto it, as being its greatest enemy, that doth more hurt than all the world besides, and the only thing that divides between our chief good and us. As this humiliation increaseth, so in the like proportion all other graces increase; for the more we are emptied of ourselves, the more we are filled with the fulness of God. The defects of this appear in the whole frame of a Christian life,

---

* The Saints' Qualification: or, a treatise—1, of humiliation, in ten sermons; 2, of sanctification, in nine sermons; whereunto is added a treatise of communion with Christ in the sacrament, in three sermons. Preached by the late faithful and worthy minister of Jesus Christ, John Preston, Doctor in Divinity, chaplain in ordinary to his majesty, master of Emmanuel College in Cambridge, and sometime preacher of Lincoln's Inn. The third edition, corrected. 'When men are cast down, then thou shalt say, There is lifting up: and he shall save the humble person,' Job xxii. 29. 'Cast away from you all your transgressions, whereby ye have transgressed, and make you a new heart, and a new spirit,' &c., Ezek. xviii. 31. 'He that eats my flesh and drinks my blood, dwelleth in me and I in him,' John vi. 56. London; Printed by R. B. for N. Bourne, and are to be sold by T. Nicholes at the Bible in Pope's-head Alley. 1637. 4to.

which is so far unsound as we retain anything of corrupted self, unhumbled for.

The foundation of Christianity is laid very low; and therefore the treatise of ' Humiliation' is well premised before that of the ' New Creature.' God will build upon nothing in us. We must be nothing in ourselves before we be raised up for a fit temple for God to dwell in, whose course is to pull down before he build. Old things must be out of request before all become new; and without this newness of the whole man from union with Christ, no interest in the new heavens can be hoped for, whereinto no defiled thing shall enter, as altogether unsuitable to that condition and place. Nothing is in request with God but this new creature, all things else are adjudged to the fire; and without this it had been better be no creature at all. By this we may judge of the usefulness of discourses tending this way. One thing more thou art to be advertised of (courteous reader), and that is, of the injurious dealing of such as for private gain have published what they can get, howsoever taken, without any acquainting either of those friends of the author's that resided in Cambridge (to whose care he left the publishing of those things that were delivered there) or of us, to whom he committed the publishing of what should be thought fit for public view of that which was preached in London. Hereby not only wrong is done to others, but to the deceased likewise, by mangling and misshaping the birth of his brain; and therefore once again we desire men to forbear publishing of anything until those that were entrusted have the review. And so we commit the treatise and thee to God's blessing.

RICHARD SIBS.
JOHN DAVENPORT.

In 1632, Sibbes introduced to the world the excellent folio of John Smith on ' The Creed,'* and the well-known and still vital treatise of John Ball on ' Faith.'† John Smith was ' preacher of the word at Clavering in Essex.' He succeeded Bishop Andrewes as lecturer in St Paul's Cathedral. Anthony Wood speaks of him as being skilled in the original languages, and well acquainted with the writings of the ablest divines. He died in November 1616.‡

* An Exposition of the Creed; or, an Explanation of the Articles of our Christian Faith. Delivered in many afternoon sermons, by that reverend and worthy divine, Master John Smith, late preacher of the Word at Clavering in Essex, and sometime Fellow of St John's College, in Oxford. Now published for the benefit and behoof of all good Christians, together with an exact table of all the chiefest doctrines and uses throughout the whole book. ' Uprightness hath boldness.' Heb. xi. 6, ' But without faith it is impossible to please him: for he that cometh unto God must believe that he is, and that he is a rewarder of them that diligently seek him.' At London: Imprinted by Felix Kyngston, for Robert Allot, and are to be sold at his shop, at the sign of the Black Bear, in Paul's Churchyard. 1632.

† A Treatise of Faith. Divided into Two Parts, the first shewing the Nature, the second the Life of Faith, both tending to direct the weak Christian how he may possess the whole word of God as his own, overcome temptations, better his obedience, and live comfortably in all estates. By John Ball. Hab. ii. 4, ' The just shall live by his faith.' The third edition, corrected and enlarged. London: Printed by Robert Young, for Edward Brewster, and are to be sold at his shop, at the sign of the Bible, upon Fleet Bridge. 1637. 4to.

‡ Wood's Athenæ (ed. by Bliss), ii. 188. And see Chalmers's Biog. Dict., sub. voce

So far as I have been able to read his folio, I must regard Sibbes's Introduction as its most valuable feature. Pearson, indeed, overshadows all such works. John Ball has been very lovingly written of by very many. Wood and Clarke, Thomas Fuller, and Richard Baxter, and Simeon Ash join in speaking 'well' of him. His books, larger and smaller, are worthy of a place beside those of Sibbes. His 'Power of Godliness' (1657), a thin folio, is marked by extraordinary acquaintance with the workings of the human heart. There are touches of weird subtlety, and one in reading can easily understand the stillness of his auditory. His treatise on 'Faith' is rich and practical.* With these few words, let us turn to the two 'epistles :'—

I. Smith on the Creed.

To the Christian Reader.

It is available, for the better entertainment of this work, to know something concerning the author, concerning the work itself, and concerning the argument; for the author, my acquaintance with him was especially towards the declining part of his years, at what time (as they speak of the sun towards setting) the light and influence which comes from worthy men is most mild and comfortable. The gifts of men then, perhaps, are not so flourishing as in their younger time, but yet more mature, and what cometh from them is better digested. In the prime of his years he was trained up in St John's College, in Oxford, being there Fellow of the House, and for piety and parts esteemed highly in the University of those that excelled in both. Afterwards he grew to that note that he was chosen to read the lecture in Paul's, succeeding therein that great, learned man, Doctor Andrewes, late Lord Bishop of Winchester, which he discharged not only to the satisfaction, but to the applause of the most judicious and learned hearers, witnessed by their frequency and attention. Not long after he was removed to a pastoral charge in Clavering, in Essex, where being fixed till his death, he shined as a star in his proper sphere.

This good man's aim was to convey himself by all manner of ways into the heart, which made him willingly heard of all sorts; for witty things only, as they are spoken to the brain, so they rest in the brain, and sink no deeper; but the heart (which vain and obnoxious men love not to be touched), that is the mark a faithful teacher aims to hit. But because the way to come to the heart is often to pass through the fancy, therefore this godly man studied by lively representations to help men's faith by the fancy. It was our Saviour Christ's manner of teaching to express heavenly things in an earthly manner; and it was the study of the wise man, Solomon, becoming a preacher, to find out pleasant words, or words of delight, Eccles. xii. 10. But when all pains are taken by the man of God, people will relish what is spoken according as their taste is. It falleth out here as it doth in a garden, wherein some walk for present delight, some carry flowers away with them to refresh them for a time; some, as bees, gather honey, which they feed on long afterwards; some, spider-like, come to suck that which may feed that malignant and venomous disposition that they bring with them. There cannot be a better character of a man than

* Consult Brook, 'Lives of the Puritans,' ii. 440, seq.

to observe what he relisheth most in hearing; for as men are, so they taste, so they judge, so they speak. Ezekiel, besides prophetical gifts fit for so high a calling, had no doubt a delightful manner of expression of himself, whereupon the wickeder sort of Jews, engaged in sinful courses, came to hear him but as a musician to please their ears, neglecting the authority of his person and the weight of his message, Ezek. xxxiii. 32. It is no wonder, therefore, if in these days people stick in the bark and neglect the pith; though sometimes it falleth out with some, as with Augustine hearing Ambrose, whilst they bite at the bait of some pleasing notions, they are, at the same time, catched with the Spirit's hook.

He was skilful in the original languages, and thereupon an excellent textman, well read in writers that were of note in the several ages of the church, which made him a well furnished and able divine. His judgment was clear and his conscience tender, and, which helped him most, he brought to the great work of the ministry an holy and gracious heart, which raised and carried him to aims above himself and the world. In his conversing he was modest, fruitful, wise, and winning; in his expressions witty and graceful, insomuch that he hath left a fresh and sweet remembrance of them to this day. Towards his end he grew more spiritual, setting light by all things here below, and only waited (as his expression was) for the coming of the Comforter; at length, his work being finished, breathing out his life with that wish of the spouse, ' Yea, come, Lord Jesus,' Rev. xxii. 20. Thus much I thought not unfit to be made known of the man.

Now, for the work itself, it must be considered by the learned reader that these things were spoken, though to a people high-raised in knowledge, and more refined than ordinary by his teaching, yet to the people, not with a purpose that they should come to the view and censure of the learned. But though they were delivered to the people, yet are they not so popular, but (if my love to the man and the work deceive me not) they will leave the best reader either more learned or more holy, or both. It must, therefore, be remembered, for the more favourable acceptation of this work, that these sermons were taken by one of his parish, a man, though pious and of good parts, yet not skilful in the learned languages; and therefore it must needs be that many apt and acute sentences of the fathers, by which this learned man did use to beautify and strengthen the points he delivered, are fallen to the ground and lost, for lack of skill to take up. But howsoever much of the spirits be lost, yet here you have the corpse and bulk of the discourse, and not without some life and vigour, wherein this is peculiar in his manner of handling, that he hath chosen fit texts of Scripture to ground his exposition of every article upon.

Now, for the argument itself, the Creed, I think it fit to premise something, because it hath been omitted by the author, or at least not gathered with the rest. The Creed is of middle authority, between divine and human, and called the Apostles' Creed, not only for consanguinity with the apostles' doctrine, but because it is taken out of the apostles' writings, and therefore of greatest authority next to the Scriptures. It is nothing else but a summary comprehension of the counsel and work of God concerning our supernatural condition here and hereafter. The doctrine of salvation is spread through the Scriptures as spirits in the arteries and blood in the veins, as the soul in the body. And here, for easier carriage, the most necessary points are gathered together, as so many pearls or precious stones, that we might have a ready use of them upon all occasions, being, as it were, a little Bible or Testament that Christians of all ranks, as suited for all conditions, may bear about with them everywhere without any trouble. In every article there is both a shallow and a depth, milk for babes and meat for strong men. Though there be no growth in regard of fundamental principles (which have been alike in all ages of the church), yet there hath and will be a proficiency in regard of conclusions drawn out of those principles. The necessities of every Christian, and the springing up of unsound opinions in the church, will continually enforce diligence and care in the further explication and application of these fundamental truths.

It will not, therefore, be amiss to set down a few directions for the more clear understanding of the Creed, and for the better making use of it. And first, for the understanding of it, it hath the name of Creed or Belief, from the act exercised about it, to shew that it doth not only contain doctrine to be believed, but that that doctrine will do us no good unless, by mingling it with our faith, we make it our belief. Therefore, both the act and the object are implied in one word, Belief. Secondly: From the execution in creation and incarnation we must arise to God's decree; nothing done in time which was not decreed before all times, ' Known unto the Lord are all his works from the beginning of the world,' Acts xv. 18. Thirdly: We must arise from one principal benefit to all that follow and accompany it, as in forgiveness of sins, follow righteousness, peace, and joy, the spirit of sanctification, Christian liberty, &c. Though the articles be nakedly propounded, yet are we to believe all the fruits and privileges. So to God's creating of heaven and earth we must join his providence in upholding and ruling all things in both. Fourthly: In the consequent we are to understand all that went before by way of cause or preparation, as in the crucifying of Christ, his preceding agony and the cause of it, our sins, and the love of God and Christ in those sufferings, &c. Fifthly: Though we are to believe circumstances as well as the thing itself, yet not with the same necessity of faith, as it is more necessary to believe that Christ was crucified than that it was under Pontius Pilate; though when any circumstance is revealed we ought to believe it, and to have a preparation of mind to believe whatsoever shall be revealed. Yet in the main points this preparation of mind is not sufficient, but there must be a present and an expressed faith. We must know that, as in the law, he that breaketh one commandment breaketh all, because all come from the same authority; so, in the grounds of faith, he that denies one in the true sense of it denies all, for both law and faith are copulatives. The singling out of anything is contrary to the obedience of faith. *Fides non eligit objectum.*

For particular and daily use, we must know, first, that every article requires a particular faith, not only in regard of the person believing, but likewise in regard of the application of the article believed; or else the devil might say the creed, for he believes there is a Creator, and that there is a remission of sins, &c.; but because he hath no share in it, it enrageth him the more. Our adversaries are great enemies to particular faith, and think we coin a thirteenth article when we enforce particular assurance, because, say they, particular men are not named in the Scripture, and what is not in Scripture cannot be a matter of faith. But there is a double faith, a faith which is the doctrine we do believe, and faith which is the grace whereby we believe; and this faith is a matter of experience wrought in our hearts by the Spirit of God. It is sufficient that that faith which we do believe is contained in the Scriptures. Now whereas they object that we make it a thirteenth article, their fourteenth apostle adds to these twelve many more articles of faith, which he enforceth to be believed, with the same necessity of faith as these twelve ; neither hath he only entered upon Christ's prerogative in minting new articles of faith, but likewise they have usurped over all Christian churches by adding Roman to the catholic church in the creed. A bold imposture!

But for special faith, the main office of the Holy Spirit is in opening general truths, to reveal our particular interest in those truths, and to breed special faith whereby we make them our own, because the Spirit of God reveals the mind of God to every particular Christian, 1 Cor. ii. 11, 12 ; for as the things believed are truths above nature, so the grace of faith whereby we believe is a grace above nature, created as a supernatural eye in the soul, to see supernatural truths.

Secondly, Where sacred truths are truly apprehended, there the Spirit works an impression in the soul suitable to the things believed ; every article hath a power in it which the Spirit doth imprint upon the soul. The belief of God to be the Father Almighty breeds an impression of dependence, reverence, and comfort. The belief and knowledge of Christ crucified is a crucifying knowledge. The true knowledge and faith in Christ rising, is a raising knowledge. The knowledge of the abasement of Christ is an abasing knowledge ; because faith sees itself one with Christ in both states. We cannot truly believe what Christ hath wrought for us, but at the same time the Spirit of Christ worketh something in us.

Thirdly, It is convenient for the giving of due honour to every person to consider of the work appropriated to every one : all come from the Father ; all are exactly performed by the Son in our nature for the redemption of those that the Father hath given him. The gathering out of the world of that blessed society (which we call the church) into an holy communion, and the sanctifying of it, and sealing unto it all the privileges believed, as forgiveness of sins, resurrection of the body, and life everlasting, &c., proceed from the Holy Ghost.

Fourthly, It has pleased the great God to enter into a treaty and covenant of agreement with us his poor creatures, the articles of which agreement are here comprised. God, for his part, undertakes to convey all that concerns our happiness, upon our receiving of them, by believing on him. Every one in particular that recites these articles from a spirit of faith makes good this condition, and this is that answer of a good conscience, which Peter speaks of, 1 Pet. iii, whereby being demanded what our faith is, every one in particular answers to every article, I believe ; I not only understand and conceive it, but assent unto it in my judgment as true, and consent to it in my will as good, and build my comfort upon it as good to me : this act of belief carries the whole soul with it.

Fifthly, Though it is we that answer, yet the power by which we answer is no less than that whereby God created the world and raised Christ from the dead. The answer is ours, but the power and strength is God's, whereby we answer, who performs both his part and ours too in the covenant. It is a higher matter to believe than the common sort think it. For this answer of faith to these truths, as it is caused by the power of God's Spirit, so is it powerful to answer all temptations of Satan, all seducements of the world, all terrors of conscience from the wrath of God and the curse of the law ; it setteth the soul as upon a rock above all.

Sixthly, These articles are a touchstone at hand to try all opinions by, for crooked things are discerned by bringing them to the rule. What directly, or by immediate and mere consequence, opposeth these, is to be rejected as contrary to the platform of wholesome doctrine. That one monster of opinions, of the bread into the body of Christ by transubstantiation, overthrows at once four articles of the Creed—the incarnation of Christ, ascension, sitting at the right hand of God, and coming to judgment; for if Christ's body be so often made of a piece of bread, being in so many places at once here upon earth, how can all these articles be true?

Again, seventhly, These grounds of faith have likewise a special influence in direction and encouragement unto all Christian duties. A holy life is but the infusion of holy truths. Augustine saith well, *Non bene vivitur, ubi bene de Deo non creditur:* men of an ill belief, cannot be of a good life; whereupon the apostles' method is, to build their exhortations to Christian duties upon the grounds of Christian faith. But we must remember, that as faith yields a good life and conscience, so a conscience is the vessel to preserve the doctrine of faith, else a shipwreck of faith will follow. If there be a delighting in unrighteousness, there will not be a love of the truth; and if we love not the truth, then there will be a preparedness to believe any lie, and that by God's just judgment, 2 Thes. ii. 12.

Eighthly. As these fundamental truths yield strength to the whole frame of a Christian life, so they are so many springs and wells of consolation for God's people to draw from; whereupon that good Prince George Anhalt (who in Luther's time became a preacher of the gospel), intending to comfort his brother Prince John, raiseth his comfort from the last three articles —remission of sins, resurrection of the body, and life everlasting; which, as they have their strength from the former articles, are able to raise any drooping spirit, and therefore in the greatest agonies it is the readiest way to suck comfort from these benefits. But I omit other things, intending only to say something by way of preface. And thus, good reader, I commend this work unto thee, and both it and thee to God's blessing.

Thine in the Lord,   R. SIBBES.

II. Ball on 'Faith.'

The Preface to the Reader.

Glorious things are spoken of the grace of graces (faith) in the Scriptures, God setting himself to honour that grace that yields up all the honour unto him in Christ: who indeed is the life of our life, and the soul of our soul. Faith only as the bond of union bringeth Christ and the soul together, and is as an artery that conveys the spirit from him as the heart, and as the sinews which convey the spirit to move all duty from him as head, whence St Paul maketh Christ's living in us, and our living by faith all one, Gal. ii. 20. Now that which giveth boldness and liberty to faith, is not only God's assignment of this office to it in the covenant of grace to come unto Christ, and unto him in Christ, to receive grace, but likewise the gracious promises whereby the great God hath engaged himself as a debtor to his poor creature, for all things needful to life and godliness, until that blessed time when we shall be put into a full possession of all things we have now only in promise, when faith shall end in fruition, and promises in performances.

Faith first looks to this word of promise, and in the promise to Christ, in whom and for whom they are yea and amen, both made and performed. And in Christ it eyeth God in whom it last resteth, as its proper centre and foundation; otherwise how should we weak sinful creatures dare to have any intercourse with God that dwelleth in that light that none can attain unto, if he had not come forth and discovered his good pleasure in Christ the substantial Word, and in the word inspired by the Holy Ghost for the good of those whom God meant for to make heirs of salvation ? Now these promises whereon all our present comfort and future hope dependeth lie hid in the Scriptures, as veins of gold and silver in the bowels of the earth, and had need be laid open, that God's people may know what upon good grounds to lay claim unto. Those, therefore, that search these mines to bring to light these treasures, deserve well of God's church. We commend (and not without cause) the witty industry of those that from springs remote bring rivers to cities, and by pipes from these rivers derive water to every man's house for all domestical services ; much more should we esteem of the religious pains of men that brings these waters of life home for every man's particular use, in all the passages and turnings of this life.

In which regard, I do not doubt, but the pains of this godly, painful, and learned man will find good entertainment of all children of the promises that hope to inherit them, who hath with great pains, and with good evidence of spiritual understanding, endeavoured to clear most matters concerning faith, and likewise discovered the variety and use of the promises, with teaching Christians how to improve their riches in Christ here spread before them, how to use the shield of faith and the sword of the Spirit upon all occasions, that so they might not only be believing but skilful Christians, knowing how to manage and make the best advantage of their faith and the word of faith. Which if they could do, there would another manner of power and beauty shine in their lives than doth. He is a man that hath formerly deserved well of the church, but in more special manner fitted for a treatise of this nature, as having been put to it to know by experience what it is to live by faith, having in sight for matters of this life very little whereupon to depend. Those that are driven to exercise their faith cannot but find God faithful, as never failing those that trust in him, they see more of God than others do.

If it be objected that others of late time have digged in the same mine and laboured in the same field, and to good purpose and success, I answer, it is true, the more this age is bound to God that directs the spirits of men to so useful, so necessary, an argument, seeing without faith we have no communion with the fountain of life, nothing in this world that can yield settled comfort to ground the soul upon, seeing without it the fairest carriage is but empty and dead morality, neither finding acceptance with God nor yielding comfort to us in our greatest extremities, and by it God himself and Christ, with all that he hath done, suffered, conquered, becometh ours and for our use. Besides, none that I know have written in our language so largely of this argument ; and such is the extent and spiritualness of this heavenly point, that many men and of the greatest graces and parts, may with great benefit to the church dive and dig still into this mystery. Neither let any except against the multitude of quotations of Scriptures ; they are brought under their proper head, and set in their proper place, and the matter itself is cut out into variety of parts. Store (as we used to speak) is no sore, we count it a delight to take out of a full heap ; the more light the conviction is the stronger ; what suits not at one time will suit our spirits and occasions at another, and what taketh not with one may take with another. But the full and well handling of matters in this treatise carries such satisfaction with it, that it frees me from necessity of further discourse, and mine own present weakness of body taketh me off. Only I was willing to yield that testimony to the fruitful pains of a faithful labourer in God's vineyard, and I judge it deserved. Receive it, therefore, Christian reader, with thanks to God that stirreth up such helpers of that faith by which we live, stand,. conquer, and in which we must die, if we look to receive the end of our faith, the salvation of our souls.

RICHARD SIBBES.

The last epistle known to me is prefixed to a very striking and suggestive book, to wit, Richard Capel's 'Treatise of Temptations.' * Nearly related to the noble family of Capel, he was yet a staunch Puritan and ' Nonconformist :' his son Daniel having also been one of the ' ejected ' of 1662. He was very much esteemed by Sibbes, who left to him a memorial ' ring ' in his will.† The book itself is well fitted to comfort the despondent, and may be placed beside Brook's 'Precious Remedies for Satan's Devices,' which it somewhat resembles, though wanting in the wonderful learning and ingenuity of illustration of that most learned and vivid of the later Puritans. The ' epistle ' follows :—

To the Christian Reader.

After the angels left their own standing, they envied ours, and out of envy became both by office and practice tempters, that they might draw man from that happy communion with God, unto that cursed condition with themselves. And success in this trade hath made them both skilful and diligent, especially now, their time being but short. And if neither the first or second Adam could be free from their impudent assaults, who then may look for exemption ? The best must most of all look to be set upon as having most of Christ in them, whom Satan hates most, and as hoping and disheartening of them, to foil others, as great trees fall not alone ; no age or rank of Christians can be free. Beginners he labours to discourage ; those that have made some progress, he raiseth storms against ; those that more perfect he labours to undermine by spiritual pride ; and above all other times, he is most busy when we are weakest, then he doubles and multiplies his forces, when he looks either to have all, or lose all. His course is either to tempt to sin or for sin. To sin, by presenting some seeming good to draw us from the true good, to seek some excellency besides God in the creature, and to this end he labours in the first place to shake our faith in the word ; thus he dealt with Adam, and thus he dealeth with all his posterity. And besides immediate suggestions, he cometh unto us, by our dearest friends, as unto Christ by Peter ; so many tempters, so many devils in that ill office, though neither they or we are oft aware of it ; the

---

* Tentations : their nature, danger, cure. By Richard Capel, sometime Fellow of Magdalen College in Oxford. The sixth edition. The fourth part left enlarged by the author, and now there is added his remains to the work of Tentations. To which thou hast prefixed an abridgment of the author's life, by Valentine Marshall, of Elmore, in Gloucestershire. 1 Cor. x. 13, There hath no tentation taken you, but such as is common to man : but God is faithful, who will not suffer you to be tempted above that you are able ; but will with the tentation also make a way to escape, that ye may be able to bear it. London : Printed by Tho. Ratcliffe, for John Bartlet, long since living in the Goldsmith's Row in Cheapside, at the Gilt Cup; since at St Austine's Gate ; now in the New buildings on the south side of Paul's near St Austine's Gate, at the sign of the Gilt Cup, and at the Gilt Cup in Westminster Hall, over against the Upper Bench. 1659.

† Consult Brook, *supra,* iii. 259 *seq.*

nearest friend of all our own flesh, is the most dangerous traitor, and therefore most dangerous because most near, more near to us than the devil himself, with which, if he had no intelligence, all his plots would come to nothing ; this holding correspondence with him, layeth us open to all danger ; it is this inward bosom enemy that doth us most mischief. When Phocas (like another Zimry) had killed his master, Mauricius the emperor, he laboured like Cain, to secure himself with building high walls, after which he heard a voice telling him, that though he built his walls never so high, yet sin within the walls would undermine all. It is true of every particular man, that if there were no tempter without, he would be a tempter to himself ; it is this lust within us that hath brought us an ill report upon the creature. This is that which makes blessings to be snares unto us ; all the corruption which is in the world is by lust, which lieth in our bosom, 2 Pet. i. 4, and as Ahithophel, or Judas, by familiarity betrayeth us, yea, oftentimes in our best affections, and actions, nature will mingle without * zeal, and privy pride will creep in, and taint our best performances with some corrupt aim. Hence it is, that our life is a continual combat. A Christian, so soon as new born, is born a soldier, and so continueth until his crown be put upon him ; in the mean time our comfort is, that ere long, we shall be out of the reach of all tentation ; ' the God of peace will tread down Satan under our feet,' Rom. xvi. 20. A carnal man's life is nothing but a strengthening and feeding of his enemy, a fighting for that which fighteth against his soul. Since Satan hath cast this seed of the serpent into our souls, there is no sin so prodigious, but some seed of it lurketh in our nature ; it should humble us to hear what sins are forbidden by Moses, which if the Holy Ghost had not mentioned, we might have been ashamed to hear of, they are so dishonourable to our nature ; the very hearing of the monstrous outrages committed by men, given up of God, as it yields matter of thanks to God for preservation of us, so of humility, to see our common nature so abused, and so abased by sin and Satan. Nay, so catching is our nature of sin, that the mention of it, instead of stirring hatred of it, often kindles fancy to a liking of it; the discovery of devilish policies and stratagems of wit, though in some respects to good purpose, yet hath no better effect in some, than to fashion their wits to the like false practices ; and the innocency of many ariseth not from the love of that which is good, but from not knowing of that which is evil.

And in nothing the sinfulness of sin appears more than in this, that it hindereth all it can, the knowledge of itself, and if it once be known, it studieth extenuation, and translation upon others ; sin and shifting came into the world together ; in St James his time, it seems that there were some that were not afraid to father their temptations to sin, upon him that hateth it most (God himself), whereas God is only said to try, not to tempt. Our adversaries are not far from imputing this to God, who maintain concupiscence, the mother of all abominations, to be a condition of nature as first created, only kept in by the bridle of original righteousness, that from hence, they might the better maintain those proud opinions of perfect fulfilling the law, and meriting thereby. This moved St James to set down the true descent and pedigree of sin ; we ourselves are both the tempters and the tempted ; as tempted we might deserve some pity, if as tempters we deserve not blame. In us there is both fire and matter for fire to take hold on. Satan needs but to blow, and oftentimes not that neither ; for many, if concupiscence stir not up them, they will stir up concupiscence. So long

* Qu. 'with our ?'—ED.

94

as the soul keeps close to God and his truth, it is safe; so long as our way lieth above, we are free from the snares below. All the danger first riseth from letting our hearts loose from God by infidelity, for then presently our heart is drawn away by some seeming good, whereby we seek a severed excellency and contentment out of God, in whom it is only to be had. After we have once forsaken God, God forsakes us, leaving us in some degree to ourselves, the worst guides that can be; and thereupon, Satan joins forces with us, setting upon us as a friend, under our own colours; he cannot but miscarry that hath a pirate for his guide. This God suffereth to make us better known to ourselves; for by this means, corruption that lay hid before, is drawn out, and the deceitfulness of sin the better known, and so we are put upon the daily practice of repentance and mortification, and driven to fly under the wings of Jesus Christ. Were it not for temptations, we should be concealed from ourselves; our graces as unexercised, would not be so bright, the power of God should not appear; so in our weakness, we would not be so pitiful and tender towards others, nor so jealous over our own hearts, nor so skilful of Satan's method and enterprises, we should not see such a necessity of standing always upon our guard; but though, by the overruling power of God, they have this good issue, yet that which is ill of itself, is not to be ventured on, for the good that cometh by accident. The chief thing wherein one Christian differs from another is watchfulness, which though it require most labour, yet it bringeth most safety; and the best is no farther safe, than watchful, and not only against sins, but tentations, which are the seeds of sin, and occasions which let in tentations. The best, by rash adventures upon occasion, have been led into temptations, and by temptation into the sin itself; whence sin and temptation come both under the same name, to shew us that we can be no further secure from sin, than we be careful to shun temptations. And in this every one should labour so well to understand themselves, as to know what they find a temptation to them. That may be a temptation to one which is not to another; Abraham might look upon the smoke of Sodom, though Lot might not; because that sight would work more upon Lot's heart than Abraham's. In these cases a wise Christian better knows what to do with himself than any can prescribe him. And because God hath our hearts in his hand, and can either suspend or give way to temptations, it should move us especially to take heed of those sins, whereby, grieving the good Spirit of God, we give him cause to leave us to our own spirits; but that he may rather stir up contrary gracious lustings in us, as a contrary principle. There is nothing of greater force to make us out of godly jealousy 'to fear always.' Thus daily 'working out our salvation,' that God may delight to go along with us, and be our shield, and not to leave us naked in the hands of Satan, but second his first grace with a further degree, as temptations shall increase. It is he that either removeth occasions, or shutteth our hearts against them, and giveth strength to prevail over them; which gracious promise you cannot be too thankful for. It is a great mercy when temptations are not above the supply of strength against them. This care only taketh up the heart of those who, having the life of Christ begun in them, and his nature stamped upon them, have felt how sweet communion and acquaintance with God in Christ, and how comfortable the daily walking with God, is; these are weary of anything that may draw away their hearts from God, and hinder their peace. And therefore they hate temptations to sin as sin itself, and sin as hell itself, and hell most of all, as being a state of eternal separation from all comfortable fellowship with God. A man that is a stranger from the life of God, cannot resist temptation to sin, as it is a sin, because he never knew the beauty of holiness ; but from the beauty of a civil life, he may resist temptations to such times * as may weaken respect, and from love of his own quiet, may abstain from those sins that will affright conscience. And the cause why civil men fear the less disturbance from temptations is, because they are wholly under the power of temptation, till God awaken their heart. What danger they see not, they feel not, the strong man holds his possession in them, and is too wise, by rousing them out of their sleep to give them occasion of thoughts of escape. None more under the danger of temptation, than they that discern it not ; they are Satan's stales, 'taken by him at his pleasure,' whom Satan useth to draw others into the same snare. Therefore Satan troubleth not them, nor himself about them ; but the true Christian fears a temptation in everything. His chief care is, that in what condition soever he be, it prove not a temptation to him. Afflictions, indeed, are more ordinarily called temptations, than prosperity, because Satan by them breedeth an impression of sorrow and fear, which affections have an especial working upon us in the course of our lives, making us often to forsake God, and desert his cause. Yet snares are laid in everything we deal with, which none can avoid but those that see them. None see, but those whose eyes God opens ; and God useth the ministry of his servants for this end, to open the eyes of men, to discover the net, and then, as the wise man saith, ' In vain is the net spread before the sight of any bird.' *Domine, quis evadet laqueos istos multos nisi videat istos ? Et quis videbit istos, nisi quem illuminaveris lumine tuo ? ipse enim pater tenebrarum laqueos suos abscondit.* Soliloq. cap. 16. Which goeth under Augustine's name. Tom. 9

This moved this godly minister, my Christian friend, to take pains in this useful argument, as appeareth in this treatise, which is written by him in a clear, quick, and familiar style ; and for the matter and manner of handling, solid, judicious, and scholar-like ; and which may commend it the more, it is written by one that, besides faithfulness and fruitfulness in his ministry, hath been a good proficient in the school of temptation himself, and therefore the fitter, as a skilful watchman, to give warning and aim to others ; for there be spiritual exercises of ministers more for others than for themselves. If by this he shall attain, in some measure, what he intended, God shall have the glory, thou the benefit, and he the encouragement to make public some other labours.—Farewell in the Lord,

RICHARD SIBBES.

These ' epistles ' and ' prefaces ' shew the cordial relations sustained by Sibbes towards his fellow-divines and contemporaries ; and down to a late period, the booksellers found it a profitable advertisement to say of a book, ' Recommended by Dr Sibbes.' †

---

* Qu. ' sins ?'—ED.

† ' Recommended by Dr Sibbes.' The various books of Preston are usually thus advertised ; and those of Burroughs, Hooker, and Cotton as ' approved by Dr Sibbes.'

CHAPTER X.

SIBBES VICAR OF TRINITY, CAMBRIDGE—PEACE-MAKER.

Presentation to Vicarage of Trinity by the King—Another relaxation of ' order' of
Gray's Inn—Lord Keeper Williams—'Tender Conscience'—'Consolatory Letter'
—Thomas Goodwin—' Summer visits'—Earls of Manchester and Warwick—
Truro and Say and Seal—Brooks and Veres—Thurston—'Mother and brethren.'

From the manner in which Sibbes escaped the practical effects
of the ' High Commission ' and ' Star-Chamber ' decisions, in striking contrast with Davenport and Hooker, and others of the fugitives
to Holland and New England, and from the fearless way in which
he continued to preach the same sentiments, it is evident that he
must have personally commanded the weightiest regard, and secured
influence that could· not be disregarded. In 1627, he passed D.D.
In 1633 (shortly after the overthrow of the ' Feoffees ' scheme,
which makes it the more memorable), he was presented by the
king, Charles I., on its resignation by Thomas Goodwin, who scarcely
held it a year,* to ' the vicarage of the holy and undivided Trinity,
in the town of Cambridge.' We have the fact in the ' Fœdera :—

' Ricardus Sibbes, clericus, in Sacra Theologia Professor, habet con-
similes Literas Patentes de presentatione ad Vicariam sanctæ et individuæ
Trinitatis in Villa Cantabrigiæ, Diocesis Eliensis, per resignationem ultimi
Incumbentis ibidem jam vacantem, et ad nostram presentationem pleno
jure spectantem ; et deriguntur hæ Literæ Reverendo in Christo Patri
Domino Francisco Eliensi Episcopo. Teste Rege apud Westmonasterium,
vicesimo primo die Novembris 1633.' †

This ' presentation' speaks much for Sibbes ; for at this date
Laud was filling every place with men of his own kind. We have
not the means of determining by what influence this appointment
was obtained. One tells us Goodwin resigned ' in favour of Sibbes,'
but that could scarcely be, inasmuch as he at the same time resigned
all his offices and honours in the University. Besides, the difficulty
is only removed back a stage ; how did it come about that a Puritan
resigned and another stepped into his place ? It may be that it was
a tacit recompence for the former injustice of ' outing ' him from his
lectureship of Trinity and his fellowship ; but it is more probable
that on the ' Feoffees'' decision, the powerful friends of the preacher
at Gray's Inn interfered in such a way as to let the primate understand that they, at any rate, were not to be trifled with ; and that
then he secured, or at least did not hinder, this ' presentation.'
But there is the further difficulty of the ' order ' of Gray's Inn,
that their preacher was not only to be continually resident, but

* Rymer's Fœdera, xix., 440, No. 81, ed. 1732.   † Ibid., xix., 536.

likewise to have no other ecclesiastical preferment. As Sibbes actually accepted and acted as vicar, the 'order' must once more have been relaxed in his favour. Indeed, I suspect that 'order' was originally passed for a personal object and from a personal reason. The immediate predecessor of Sibbes was a Mr Fenton,— in all likelihood, though no Christian name appears in the 'Order-Books' of Gray's Inn, the same with Roger Fenton, D.D., who was a great pluralist, and who died 16th January 1615–16. He held the prebend, rectory, and vicarage of St Pancras, and the rectory of St Stephen's, Walbrook, and also the vicarage of Chigwell, Essex, till his death. Probably he neglected his duties as preacher at Gray's Inn. Hence the check put upon his successor.* For one so faithful in the discharge of his office, and who was regarded by all as a personal friend, there would be no great difficulty in making arrangements, in order to his accepting the 'presentation,' and still continuing the honoured preacher of Gray's Inn.

It is greatly to be lamented that the most diligent and persistent research has failed to add any memorials to the fact of his entrance on the vicarage of Trinity. Though he must have been non-resident, he would have many opportunities to officiate during 'vacation' time at the Inn.

This is the last public honour recorded as having been conferred upon Sibbes. What remains to be told partakes of the privacy of his daily life.

One little fact, half-casually recorded in that extraordinary folio, 'Scrinia Reserata: a Memorial offer'd to the great deservings of John Williams, D.D., who some time held the place of Lord Keeper of the Great Seal of England, &c., &c., &c., by John Hacket, late Lord Bishop of Litchfield and Coventry,' 1693—a book *sui generis*, and than which none gives profounder insight into the 'form and pressure of the age,'—brings out a very beautiful side of Sibbes's character, and dates to us, if I err not, one of the most interesting, biographically, of his minor writings. Vindicating Williams—a vindication which, the more successful it is, the more it damages the strangely contradictory character of the Lord Keeper —from the rumour of favouring Puritans, Hacket thus introduces Sibbes :—

'Another rank for whose sake the Lord Keeper suffer'd, were scarce an handful, not above three or four in all the wide Bishoprick of Lincoln, who did not oppose, but by an ill education seldom used the appointed ceremonies. Of whom when he was certified by his commissaries and officials.

* 'Check put upon his successor.' For these facts and the inference from them I owe thanks to Dr Hessey

he sent for them, and confer'd with them with much meekness, sometimes remitted them to argue with his chaplain. If all this stirred them not, *he commended them to his old collegiate Dr Sibbes,* or Dr Gouch (Gouge), *who knew the scruples of these men's hearts,* and how to bring them about, the best of any about the city of London.'*

There is such a fascination, spite of all his errors, or it may be crimes, about the hot-blooded Welshman, so stormy and impulsive, so wise and yet so foolish, that one is glad to find, that even when he was 'Lord Keeper,' and surrounded by very different men, he forgot neither him who was once his humble fellow-student of St John's, nor the staunch puritan of ' Blackfryers,' William Gouge, also a contemporary at Cambridge, but—

> ' They had been friends, when friendship is
> A passion and a blessedness ;
> And in a tender sacrament
> Unto the house of God they went,
>   And plighted love,—caressing
>   The same dear cup of blessing.

> ' They had been friends in youth, most dear ;
> In studious night, and mirthful cheer,
> And high discourse, and large debate,
> Unmixed by bitterness or hate—
>   Their fellowship, I ween,
>   A pleasant thing had been.'

It is specially pleasing to know what was the occasion of again associating the students of earlier years—to wit, tender dealing with tender consciences. I like to place that over against his after humiliating repudiation of all Puritans, extorted from him while under the shadow of a charge of treason, and in a letter to LAUD.† He was truthful in his favour ; untruthful in his disfavour. The fact also dates, as I have intimated, one of the minor writings of Sibbes, which illustrates how he would discharge the office assigned to him. It is entitled :—

A CONSOLATORY LETTER To an afflicted Conscience : full of pious admonitions and Divine Instructions. Written by that famous Divine, Doctor SIBBS : and now published for the common good and edification of the Church. Ecclesiastes vi. 18, *Be not thou just overmuch, neither make thy selfe overwise ; wherefore shouldest thou be desolate.*
[Woodcut portrait. Ætat: Suæ 58.] London, Printed for *Francis Coules. 1641.* ‡

* i. 95. ' Scrinia ' seems to have been a favourite title. The historical student will recall also ' Scrinia Ceciliana.'

† Works of Laud. vi. pp. 312-314. Sept. 9. 1633.

‡ For a copy of this excessively rare ' Letter,' published in a thin 4to, pp. 6, I am indebted to the kindness of Joshua Wilson, Esq., Nevill Park, Tunbridge Wells, who has devoted much time to good purpose in investigating the history, and biography, and bibliography of Puritanism. His ' Historical Inquiry concerning the Principles, &c., of English Presbyterians ' (1835) has not gathered all its renown yet.

I introduce this 'Letter' here, retaining its orthography :—

Deare Sir,

I understand by your Letter, that you have many and great tryals ; some externall and bodily, some internall and spirituall : as the deprivall of inward comfort, the buffetings (and that in more then ordinary manner), of your soule, with Satans temptations : and (which makes all those inward and outward, the more heavy and insupportable) that you have wanted Christian society with the Saints of God, to whom you might make knowne your griefes, and by whom you might receive comfort from the Lord, and incouragement in your Christian course.

Now that which I earnestly desire in your behalfe, and hope likewise you doe in your owne, is that you may draw nearer to God, and be more conformable to his command by these afflictions ; for if our afflictions be not sanctified, that is, if we make not an holy use of them by purging out the old leaven of our ingenerate corruptions, they are but judgments to us, and makes way for greater plagues : Ioh v. 14. And therefore the chiefe end and ayme of God in all the afflictions which he sends to his children in love, is, that they may be partakers of his holinesse, and so their afflictions may conduce to their spirituall advantage and profit, Heb. xii. 10. The Lord aymes not at himselfe in any calamities he layes on us, (for God is so infinitely all-sufficient, that we can adde nothing to him by all our doings or sufferings) but his maine ayme is at our Melioration and Sanctification in and by them. And therefore our duty in every affliction and pressure, is thus to thinke with our selves : How shall we carry and behave our selves under this crosse, that our soules may reap profit by it ? This (in one word) is done by our returning and drawing nearer to the Lord, as his holy Apostle exhorts us, Iames iv. 8. This in all calamities the Lord hath a speciall eye unto, and is exceeding wroth if he finde it not.

The Prophet declares *That his anger was not turned from Israel, because they turned not to him that smote them,* Isa. i. 4, 5. Now it is impossible that a man should draw nigh to God, and turne to him, if he turne not from his evill wayes : for in every conversion there is *Terminus à quo,* something to be turned from, as well as *Terminus ad quod,* something to be turned to.

Now, that we must turn to, is God ; and that we must turne from, is sinne ; as being diametrally opposite to God, and that which separates betweene God and us.

To this purpose we must search and try our hearts and wayes, and see what sinnes there be that keepe us from God, and separate us from his gracious favour : and chiefly we must weed out our speciall bosom-sins. This the ancient Church of God counsels each other to doe in the time of their anguish and affliction, Lam. iii. 39, 40, *Let us search and try our wayes, and turne againe to the Lord :* for though sinne make not a finall divorce betwixt God and his chosen people, yet it may make a dangerous rupture by taking away sense of comfort, and suspending the sweet influence of his favour, and the effectuall operation of his grace.

And therefore (deare Sir) my earnest suit and desire is, that you would diligently peruse the booke of your conscience, enter into a thorow search and examination of your heart and life ; and every day before you goe to bed, take a time of recollection and meditation, (as holy *Isaac* did in his private walkes, Gen. xxiv. 63), holding a privy Session in your soule, and indicting your selfe for all the sins, in thought, word, or act committed, & all the good duties you have omitted. This self-examination, if it be so strict and rigid as it ought to be, will soone shew you the sins whereto you

are most inclinable (the chiefe cause of all your sorrowes), and conse-
quently, it will (by God's assistance) effectually instruct you to fly from
those venomous and fiery serpents, which have so stung you.

And though you have (as you say) committed many grievous sinnes, as
abusing God's gracious ordinances, and neglecting the golden opportunities
of grace : the originall, as you conceive of all your troubles ; yet I must tell
you, there is another *Coloquintida* in the pot, another grand enormity
(though you perceive it not) and that is your separation from Gods Saints
and Servants in the Acts of his publike Service and worship. This you
may clearly discern by the affliction it selfe, for God is methodicall in his
corrections, and doth (many times) so suite the crosse to the sinne, that
you may reade the sin in the crosse. You confesse that your maine affliction, and that which made the other more bitter, is, that God tooke away
those to whom you might make your complaint ; and from whom you
might receive comfort in your distresse. And is not this just with God,
that when you wilfully separate your selfe from others, he should separate
others from you ? Certainly, when we undervalue mercy, especially so
great a one as the communion of Saints is, commonly the Lord takes it
away from us, till we learne to prize it to the full value. Consider well
therefore the haynousnesse of this sin, which that you may the better conceive,
First, consider it is against Gods expresse Precept, charging us not to forsake the assemblies of the Saints, Heb. x. 20, 25. Again, it is against
our own greatest good and spirituall solace, for by discommunicating &
excommunicating our selves from that blessed society, we deprive our
selves of the benefit of their holy conference, their godly instructions, their
divine consolations, brotherly admonitions, and charitable reprehensions ;
and what an inestimable losse is this ? Neither can we partake such profit
by their prayers as otherwise we might : for as the soule in the naturall
body conveyes life and strength to every member, as they are compacted
and joyned together, and not as dis-severed ; so Christ conveyes spirituall
life and vigour to Christians, not as they are disjoyned from, but as they
are united to the mysticall body, the Church.

But you will say *England* is not a true Church, and therefore you
separate ; adhere to the true Church.

I answer, our Church is easily proved to be a true Church of Christ :
First, because it hath all the essentialls, necessary to the constitution of a
true Church ; as sound preaching of the Gospell, right dispensation of the
Sacraments, Prayer religiously performed, and evill persons justly punisht
(though not in that measure as some criminals and malefactors deserve :)
and therefore a true Church.

2. Because it hath begot many spirituall children to the Lord, which for
soundnesse of judgement, and holinesse of life, are not inferiour to any in
other Reformed Churches. Yea, many of the Separation, if ever they
were converted, it was here with us : (which a false and adulterous Church
communicated.)

But I heare you reply, our Church is corrupted with Ceremonies, and
pestered with prophane persons. What then ? must we therefore separate
for Ceremonies, which many think may be lawfully used. But admit they
be evils, must we make a rent in the Church for Ceremonious Rites, for
circumstantiall evils ? That were a remedy worse than the disease. Besides, had not all the true Churches of Christ their blemishes and deformi-
ties, as you may see in seaven *Asian* Churches ? Rev. ii. and iii. And
though you may finde some Churches beyond Sea free from Ceremonies,

yet notwithstanding they are more corrupt in Preachers, (which is the maine) as in prophanation of the Lord's day, &c.

As for wicked and prophane Persons amongst us, though we are to labour by all good meanes to purge them out, yet are we not to separate because of this residence with us : for, there will bee a miscellany and mixture in the visible Church, as long as the world endures, as our Saviour shewes by many parables : Matth. xiii. If therefore we should be so overjust as to abandon all Churches for the intermixture of wicked Persons, we must saile to the Antipodes, or rather goe out of the world, as the Apostle speaks : it is agreed by all that *Noahs* Arke was a type and embleme of the Church. Now as it had been no lesse then selfe-murder for *Noah, Sem,* or *Iaphet,* to have leapt out of the Arke, because of that ungracious *Cains* * company ; so it is no better then soule-murder for a man to cast himself out of the Church, either for reall or imaginall corruptions. To conclude, as the Angell injoyned *Hagar* to returne, and submit to her Mistris *Sarah,* so let me admonish you to returne your selfe from these extravagant courses, and submissively to render your self to the sacred communion of this truly Evangelicall Church of *England.*

I beseech you therefore, as you respect Gods glory and your owne eternall salvation, as *There is but one body and one spirit, one Lord, one Baptisme, one God and Father of all, who is above all, and through all, and in us all ; so endeavour to keep the unity of the spirit in the bond of peace,* Eph. iv., as the Apostle sweetly invites you. So shall the peace of God ever establish you, and the God of peace ever preserve you ; which is the prayer of

Your remembrancer at the Throne of Grace R. SIBS.

The preceding 'Letter,' the more valuable because of the paucity of such memorials of Sibbes, was in all likelihood addressed to Thomas Goodwin, D.D., who has been designated the Atlas and patriarch of Independency. Francis White, Bishop of Ely, within whose jurisdiction the Church of Trinity, Cambridge, lay, being one of the ultra-zealous adherents of Laud, had put every obstacle possible in the way of Goodwin's acceptance, and subsequently of his installation ; but he was ultimately installed as vicar, having passed from the curacy of St Andrew's, Cambridge, thereto. On the succession of Laud to the primacy, his special charge to his bishops was to watch over the lecturers, and 'watch over' had a terrible significance. White harassed all within his diocese who sought to preach evangelically. He renewed his attacks upon Goodwin. The result was, that, dissatisfied with the restrictions imposed upon preaching that truth which, from the time of Sibbes's barbed words to him, he had found to be the very life of his own soul, he resigned at once his vicarage, lectureship of Trinity, and fellowship of Catharine Hall, and removed, as it would appear, to London, where he began to propagate his new views and conclusions in regard to church government. He shrank not from the name, then of evil omen, of 'Separatist.' † The

* Qu. 'Cham's ?'—ED.

† Consult Dr Halley's Memoir of Goodwin in this series, II, xxiii–iv.

whole circumstances of the case, their previous friendship, their mutual sentiments, warrant, I apprehend, the supposition that this grave, loving, skilful, and admirable letter was addressed to Thomas Goodwin. If so, it was unsuccessful in winning him back to 'the church.' Methinks Sibbes would have acted more faithfully as well as more consistently, had he followed the example of his friends, Goodwin, John Cotton, John Davenport, Thomas Hooker, Samuel Stone, and their compeers. The spirit that pervades his letter is worthier than his arguments. It seems difficult to see how Goodwin could have remained within the pale of the church, gagged and hindered as he was in what was to him momentous beyond all earthly estimate; and it was equally impossible to give 'assent and consent' to what those in authority pronounced to be the 'beauty of holiness,' and teaching of the Book of Common Prayer. Sibbes allowed of neither. By the powerful influence of his many friends, while certainly, as we have seen, summoned before Star Chamber and High Commission, he held on in his way of preaching the same gospel everywhere. That explains his remaining within the church. Who doubts for a moment, that, if his mouth had been shut, as was Goodwin's, on the 'one thing,' Sibbes would have placed himself beside his friend? Perhaps there would have been more of lingering effort to get above the difficulties, more pain in sundering of the ties that bound him to the church, more sway given to heart than head. Still the final decision, beyond all debate, would have been that of the 'two thousand' of 1662. The more shame to those who compelled such loyal lovers of 'the church' to leave her. This letter gives us insight into Sibbes's method of procedure in dealing with the scruples of the conscientious. It is to be regretted that we have no more of such letters, and none of his conversations with them. But we have the fact, upon various authority, that he was at all times ready to speak a word in season, and on principle, contrived to *sanctify* all his intercourse with his fellow-men, as well more privately as publicly. He had many opportunities of influencing for good some of the finest minds of the age; and he availed himself of such opportunities. He was wont, Samuel Clarke informs us, 'in the summer time, to go abroad to the houses of some worthy personages, *where he was an instrument of much good*, not only by his private labours, but by his prudent counsel and advice, that upon every occasion he was ready to minister unto them.' * Charles Stanford has well limned to us such visits in Alleine's day. If you wish, he says, 'to see what Puritan life was like in "the high places," go with Mr Alleine and

* Clarke, *ante*, p. 145.

his brother Norman, to spend an evening with Admiral Blake at his country house at Knowle.'* Instead of Alleine let us go with Sibbes, and instead of Admiral Blake at Knowle, let the visit be to John Pym, or to Lady Mary Vere, or to Sir Robert and Lady Brooke, or any of those great and true families, whose heads

> '. . . . . bore, without abuse,
> The grand old name of gentleman,'

and 'feared God,' and were 'lovers of all good men.' Suppose Colonel Hutchinson and the Puritan Admiral to be also guests. There would be the simple meal,—the Bible would be brought in, —there would be prayer,—there would be conversation such as Christians love, and which they can only have when in 'their own company,'—there would probably be discourse, in logical forms, on some of the mysteries of Christian truth,—of course, there would be reasonings over some 'case of conscience.' Dr Gouge would be apt to get prosy, in discussing the opinions of Fragosa, Talet, Sayrus, and Roderiques, or of Doctors Ursinus or Lobetius; Master Davenport would interpose a 'why' or 'how;' and Richard Sibbes would close with some sweet words from John or the Lord himself, modestly confirming his own elucidations of them from Bernard, or with a quaint saying from Luther, or a wise apophthegm from Augustine. Then there would be a flow of graceful and varied talk, not only on politics ('Petition of Right,' and so on), but on books, pictures, gardening, or the last scientific experiments of the 'Oxford Society;' and the tall-browed statesman, and the great sailor, 'would affect a droll concern to prove before the ministers, by the aptness and abundance of their Latin quotations, that in becoming 'leader in the House' and admiral, they had not forfeited their claim to be considered good classics.' You could not find better types of the winning, yet stately Christian gentleman, than among such Puritan circles; and where will you match their 'fair ladyes?' We have confirmation of the 'visits' and of their results in the several 'epistles' and 'dedications' of his posthumous writings. Each of these records personal intercourse and kindnesses, and the tenderest cherishing of his memory. He was a frequent guest with the Earls of Manchester and Warwick, and Ladies Anne and Susanna, their Countesses, Lord Say and Seal, Lord Roberts, Baron Truro, and Lady Lucie his consort, but most of all with the Brooks and Veres, with whom he lived on the most familiar terms. The 'dedications' and 'epistles' will be found in their respective

---

* Joseph Alleine: his Companions and Times, pp. 131-2; and Hepworth Dixon's Life of Blake, p. 267. I accommodate, rather than quote from Stanford's picturesque and masterly work.

places; but, as it reflects interesting light and mutual honour on both, I must introduce in full the ' epistle dedicatory' of the 'Fountain Sealed,' to 'the truly noble and much honoured lady, the Lady Elizabeth Brooke, wife to Sir Robert Brooke,' and also glean a few biographic sentences from others. The 'epistle' to Lady Brooke, one of the most remarkable women of England, at a period when there were many such, is as follows :—

To the truly noble and much honoured lady, the LADY ELIZABETH BROOKE, *wife to Sir Robert Brooke.*

' Madam,—Besides that deserved interest your Ladyship held in the affections and esteem of this worthy man more than any friend alive, which might entitle you to all that may call him author, this small piece of his acknowledgeth a more special propriety unto your Ladyship. For though his tongue was as the pen of a ready writer in the hand of Christ, who guided him, yet your Ladyship's hand and pen was in this his scribe and amanuensis, whilst he dictated a first draught of it in private, with intention for the public. In which labour, both of humility and love, your Ladyship did that honour unto him which Baruch, though great and noble, did but receive in the like transcribing the words of Jeremiah from his mouth, wherein yet your Ladyship did indeed but write the story of your own life, which hath been long exactly framed to the rules herein prescribed. We, therefore, that are intrusted in the publishing of it, deem it but an act of justice in us to return it thus to your Ladyship, unto whom it owes even its first birth, that so, wherever this little treatise shall come, there also this that you have done may be told and recorded for a memorial of you. And we could not but esteem it also an addition of honour to the work, that no less than a lady's hand, so pious and so much honoured, brought it forth into the world, although in itself it deserveth as much as any other this blessed womb did bear. The Lord, in way of recompense, write all the holy contents of it yet more fully and abundantly in your ladyship's heart, and all the lineaments of the image of Jesus Christ, and seal up all unto you by his blessed Spirit, with joy and peace, to the day of redemption.— Madam, we are your Ladyship's devoted,   THOS. GOODWIN.
      PHILIP NYE.

It was no uncommon thing for ladies moving in the highest circles thus to 'take down' the sermons of their ministers, or discharge the office of amanuenses. Contemporaneously with Lady Brooke we find Lady Elizabeth Rich, another of Sibbes's friends, transcribing and preparing for the press WILLIAM STRONG'S great folio ' Of the Covenants.'* Of Lady Brooke, her biographer Parkhurst states, among many other things of note, that—

' She used a mighty industry to preserve what either instructed her mind or affected her heart in the sermons she had heard. To these she gave great attention in the Assembly, and heard them repeated in her family. And thus she would discourse of them in the evening; and in the following week she had them again repeated, and discoursed the matter of them to some of her family in her chamber. And besides all this, *she wrote the substance of them,* and then digested many of them into questions and

* 1678. Dedication by Theophilus Gale to Lady Elizabeth Rich.

answers, or under heads of common-places, and then they became to her matter for repeated meditation. And by these methods she was always increasing her knowledge, or confirming the things that were known.'*

Addressing Lord Roberts, Baron Truro, and Lady Lucie, John Sedgwick thus commences his 'dedication' of the 'Beams of Divine Light:'—

' RIGHT HONOURABLE AND TRULY NOBLE,—It was not so much the nobility of your blood, as that of grace given unto you from the divine hand, *which did so much interest you in the love and esteem of that worthy servant of Christ*, the author of this work, in whom Urim and Thummim met, whose whole course being a real and vital sermon, sweetly consonant to the tenor of his teaching, made him amiable living and honourable dead, in the opinion of as many as well knew him. This was the thing, I suppose, which wrought unto him from you, *as well as from many others of your noble stock and rank*, more than an ordinary esteem.' †

Again, in like manner he addresses Robert, Earl of Warwick, and Lady Susanna, in ' Light from Heaven:'—

' For me to commend the author, were to make the world to judge him either *a stranger unto you, or a man that had not ingratiated himself with you whilst he lived near unto you.* I well knew that he had an honourable opinion of you both, and of yours. . . . . You that knew and loved him so well shall, in vouchsafing to read over these ensuing sermons, find his spirit in them.' ‡

These ' testimonies' might be greatly multiplied, and it is very pleasing to know that one who so carried about with him the ' sweet savour' of Christ was thus welcomed at the Kimboltons, and Cockfields, and Hevinghams, and other of the family seats and castles of the nobility and gentry. It is especially honourable to Sibbes that he received such cordial welcome from the nobles and gentry of his own native county of Suffolk. The Tostock ' wheelwright's' son reversed the too often true saying of a prophet not being without honour ' save in his own country and among his own kin.' The Day will declare the good effected by these summer visits and ' conferences in private, done aptly, pithily, and profitably . . . . much in few words.' §

While thus a visitor among the ' great ones,' he did not forget his birth-place or school-boy haunts, his ' mother, and brethren.' I turn here to the manuscript of the Vicar of Thurston :—

' Anno Domini 1608. I came to be minister of Thurston, and he was then a Fellow of the College, and a preacher of good note in Cambridge, and we soon grew well acquainted. For whensoever he came down into the

* Quoted in Wilford's ' Memorials and Characters,' folio, 1741, page 210. Consult pp. 209-213, and Appendix xvii.
† Ep. Ded., 4to, 1639. ‡ Ep. Ded., 4to, 1638.
§ ' Epistle Dedicatory' to ' Evangelical Sacrifices,' 4to, 1640.

country to visit his mother and brethren (his father being deceased) he would never fail to preach with us on the Lord's day, and for the most part twice, telling me that it was a work of charity to help a constant and a painful preacher, for so he was pleased to conceive of me. And if there were a communion appointed at any time he would be sure not to withdraw himself after sermon, but receiving the bread and wine at my hands, he would always assist me in the distribution of the cup to the congregation.'

The church of Thurston, in which Sibbes thus ministered, has only within these two years disappeared. Its great tower fell, and it was found necessary to rebuild the whole. This has been done nearly in fac-simile of the original.* The parsonage of the excellent vicar remains. It has degenerated into a kind of farmer's house, but on a recent visit I found many traces of former elegance and comfort. It is two-storied, with lozenge-paned windows, and heavy sculptured doorway. In front is an avenue of noble chesnuts and beeches, and pollard limes. The 'garden' must have been of considerable extent. Imagination was busy calling up Sibbes and Catlin walking arm-in-arm along the mossed avenue. I stepped across the threshold of the ancient house, sat down by the carved mantel-pieced fireside with reverence. It was something to know that there our worthies had many and many a time exchanged loving words, perhaps smoked a pipe.

Finely does the vicar continue his personal reminiscences of the visits to Thurston, and of his friend's kindnesses. We must again listen to him :—

' As for his kindness to his kindred, and neglect of the world, it was very remarkable. For this I can testify of my own knowledge, that, purchasing of Mr Tho. Clark and others in our town a messuage and lands at several times to the value of fifty pounds per annum, he paid the fines to the lords but never took one penny of the rents or profits of them, *but left the benefit wholly to his mother and his two brethren* as long as he lived. So much did this heavenly-minded man of God' ('heavenly' seems instinctively to drop from every one who writes of him) ' slight this present world (which the most men are so loth to part withal when they die) that he freely and undesired parted with it whilst he lived, requiring nothing of them but only to be liberal to the poor. Nay, over and besides, if any faithful, honest man came down from Cambridge or London, where he lived, by whom he might conveniently send, he seldom or never failed to *send his mother* a

* An engraving of the church as it was before its fall is given in one of those privately printed family histories, for which we are indebted to the love of the Americans towards their mother country. ' The Brights of Suffolk, England ; represented in America by the descendants of Henry Bright jun., who came to New England in 1630, and settled in Watertown, Massachusetts. By J. B. Bright. For private circulation. Boston. 1 vol. royal 8vo. 1858.' See opposite page 109. This book is of the deepest interest, well arranged, and illustrated lavishly with portraits and other illustrations.'

piece of gold, for the most part a ten shilling piece, but five shillings was the least,* and this he continued as long as his mother lived. And would she have been persuaded to exchange her country life for the city, he often told me that he would willingly have maintained her there in good view and fashion, *like his mother*, but she had no mind to alter her accustomed course of life in her old days, contenting herself with her own means, and that addition which her son made thereunto.'

And still farther the good old man continues, with a love and reverence most affecting, and that only a *true* man could have secured :—

' For his special kindness to myself, in particular, I cannot omit that, being trusted by personages of quality with divers sums of money for pious and charitable uses, he was pleased, among many others, not to forget me. At one time he sent me down three twenty-shilling pieces of gold enclosed in a letter, and at two other times he delivered to me with his own hand two twenty-shilling pieces more ; and so far was this humble saint from pharisaical ostentation and vainglory, and from taking the honour of these good works to himself, that he plainly told me that these gratuities were not of his own cost, but being put in trust, and left to his own discretion in the distribution, he looked upon me as one that took great pains in my ministry and in teaching scholars, and at that time labouring under the burden of a great charge of children, and so thought me a fit object of their intended charity. And from myself his love descended down to my son for my sake, for whom (before he had ever seen him, being then at the grammar-school at Bury, he then, chosen Master of Katherine Hall, promised me a scholarship there of five pounds a year, and to provide for him a tutor and a chamber. And such was his constancy of spirit and his reality, that whatsoever promise he made me he would be sure both to remember it and to make it good as freely as he first made it, that was unasked and undesired. And for these manifold kindnesses all that he desired at my hands was no more but this, *that I would be careful of the souls of my people, and, in special, of his mother, his brethren, and his sisters*, and would give them good counsel in their disposing themselves in marriage, or upon any other occasion, as I saw they stood in need. And this one thing I may not pass over concerning myself, that in his last will and testament he gave me a legacy of forty shillings, with the title of " his loving friend," which I the rather mention, because I had not the least thought to have been in that sort remembered by him at his death, living at no less distance from him than of threescore miles. In a word, such was the lowliness of this sweet servant of God, such his learning, parts, piety, prudence, humility, sincerity, love, and meekness of spirit (whereof every one was a loadstone to attract, unite, and fasten my spirit close to his), that I profess ingenuously no man that ever I was acquainted withal got so far into my heart or lay closer there, so that many times I could not part from him with dry eyes. But who am I ? or what is it to be beloved of me, *especially for him that had so many and great friends as he had ?* Yet even to me the great God is pleased to say, " My son, give me thy heart," and this poor and contrite heart I know he will not despise; and this heart of mine, as small as it is, yet is too great to close with a proud, profane, worldly, malicious heart, though it be in a prince. But true virtue and

* This may fairly be considered equal to a pound of our present money.

grace are the image of God himself, and where they are discerned by wisdom's children they command the heart and are truly lovely and venerable,
whereas carnal notions and unmortified affections (whereof this man of God
was as free as any man I know living), they do render a man, whatever he
be, if not hateful and contemptible, yet at least less lovely and honourable.
But my love to this good man hath transported me beyond my purpose,
which was to speak of some things less visible to others, especially concerning his first education. For when he came to the university and the
city, there his life and actions were upon a public theatre, and his own
words, without a trumpet, would praise him in the gates. As for his kindness to his kindred and to myself, I know none that took more notice of
them than I, and therefore I could not hide them from the world upon
this occasion without some kind of sacrilege.'

Thanks, chatty Zachary, for thy golden words! Thou wert a
meet companion of Richard Sibbes! Would that we might recover
thy ' Hidden Treasure,' * for, of a truth, it must breathe thy very
spirit! All the notices of the author of The Bruised Reed and
Soul's Conflict harmonise with the tribute of the vicar of Thurston.
Whether it be Clark or Thomas Fuller, Prynne or Eachard, or his
numerous ' prefacers,' he is invariably spoken of with the most
touching kindliness.

CHAPTER XI.

'THE BEGINNING OF THE END.'

Retrospect—Character—Humility—the English Leighton—his ' Cygnea-Cantio '
vel Concio.

We have now reached ' the beginning of the end.' A few months
later, and Richard Sibbes lay dying. But at this point, I would
observe, that up to the latest he continued faithfully to execute his
office as a ' preacher of the word.' Left alone (for Preston was gone:
and Cotton, and Davenport, and Hooker, and many others of his
circle, were fugitives in New England), he had ever-increasing de-
mands made upon him, and no ' door of entrance' was opened into
which he did not enter, still

' Hoping through the darkest day.' †

He continued to preach at Gray's Inn, in the good old way, the
simple gospel that Paul preached, and that of all men JOHN CAL-
VIN, following Augustine, in his estimate, had best interpreted.

* The following is the title, from Crowe's Catalogue of our English writers on
Old and New Testament, &c., 1668 :—' Hidden-Treasure, two sermons on Mat.
xiii. 44. 4to. 1633.' Can any reader help to this?
† Poems by Currer, Ellis, and Acton Bell, p. 34, 12mo. 1846.

He resided with enlarged acceptability as Master of Catharine Hall, adding to its Fellows, and Students, and Revenues, and from 1632–3, he was, as already recorded, Vicar of Trinity, Cambridge. One incidental sentence informs us, that he was very fully, if not over, occupied, even before his presentation to the Vicarage of Trinity. It occurs at the close of the address ' To the Christian Reader' prefixed to ' The Bruised Reed :' ' What I shall be drawn to do in this kind,' he says, ' *must be by degrees, as leisure in the midst of many interruptions will permit.'*

His was a self-sacrificing, self-consuming life. Quaintly does Mather put it of another. ' There,' he says, ' 'twas that, like a silk-worm, he spent his own bowels or spirits to procure the " garments of righteousness" for his hearers ; there 'twas . . . he might challenge the device and motto of the famous Dr Sibs, a wasting lamp, with this inscription, " *Prælucendo pereo,*" or, " My light is my death." '*

Another casual reference indicates earlier personal sickness. He closes one of his ' Epistles ' prefixed to Ball† by saying, ' Mine own weakness of body taketh me off.'

His published writings afford the best evidence of what stamp his preaching was. The most cursory reader is struck with the Paul-like kindling of emotion, the Paul-like burning of utterance, as often as the name of Christ occurs ; and it is most interesting to mark the majestic procession of his words as he walks along some great avenue of thought, leading up to the cross, and from the cross, in farther vista, to the house of many mansions, and to the throne of sculptured light. Very beautifully does Clarke put this:—

His learning was mixed with humility, whereby he always esteemed lowly of himself, and was ready to undervalue his own labours, though others judged them to breathe spirit and life, to be strong of heaven, speaking with authority and power to men's consciences. His care in the course of his ministry was to lay a good ,foundation in the heads and hearts of his hearers. And though he were a wise master-builder, and that in one of the eminentest auditories for learning and piety that was in the land, as was said before, yet according to the grace which was given to him (which was indeed like that of Elisha in regard of the other prophets, 2 Kings i. 9, the elder brother's privilege, a double portion), *he was still taking all occasions to preach of the* FUNDAMENTALS *to them :* and amongst the rest, of the incarnation of the Son of God, one of the chief fundamentals of our faith, one of the chief of those wonders in the mercy-seat which the cherubim gaze at, which the angels desire to pry into, 1 Pet. i. 12. And preaching at several times, and by occasion of so many several texts of Scripture concerning this subject, there is scarce any one of those incomparable benefits which accrue to us thereby, nor any of those holy impressions which the meditation hereof ought to make on our hearts, which was not by him

* Life of Urian Oakes. Magnalia Am. as *ante,* b. iv. pp. 186, 187.   † *Ante* p. cvi.

sweetly unfolded, as may appear by those sermons now in print. ' And therefore,' saith a reverend divine, ' the *noted humility of the author* I less wonder at, finding how often his thoughts dwelt upon the humiliation of Christ.'*

The ' reverend divine' referred to was Thomas Fuller, who plays with the conceit in his own wisely-witty way. We cannot pass it by :—

He was most eminent for that grace which is most worth, yet costs the least to keep it, viz., *Christian humility.* Of all points of divinity, he most frequently pressed that of Christ's incarnation ; and if the angels desired to pry into that mystery, no wonder if this angelical man had a longing to look therein. A learned divine imputed this good doctor's great humility to his much meditating on that point of Christ's humiliation when he took our flesh upon him. If it be true what some hold in physic, that *omne par nutrit suum par*, that the vitals of our body are most strengthened by feeding on such meats as are likest unto them, I see no absurdity to maintain that men's souls improve most in those graces whereon they have most constant meditation, whereof this worthy doctor was an eminent instance.†

Aye, quaint and loveable Fuller, and there is a higher authority than ' physic' for it, even 2 Cor. iii. 18, ' We all, with open face beholding as in a glass the glory of the Lord, *are changed into the same image* from glory to glory, even of the Lord, the Spirit.'

Thus growing in holiness and humility, Richard Sibbes passed along his ' pilgrimage.' We have found that he lived in troublous times, and that he did not escape his own share of its trials and persecution. It had argued time-serving or a cold neutrality had it been otherwise. We find him also taking a fitting stand for ' the truth,' and speaking brave and noble words, and flinching not from giving them to the world. At the same time, it must be apparent to all who have followed our memoir thus far, that naturally Sibbes was of a ' meek and quiet spirit,' willing to bear and forbear much. I picture him as an English ' Leighton,' as *he* has been pourtrayed in a little volume of ' poems,' entitled ' The Bishop's Walk.'‡ We have to change very little in the scenery, have but to translate ' Dunblane' to the ' fair garden' lined with elms, of Gray's Inn, or to the acacia-bordered ' Walk' of St Catherine Hall, Cambridge, or, perhaps, to the bosky glades of the Veres, or Brooks, or Manchesters, or Warwicks. I invite my readers to judge :—

* Clarke, *ante* p. 144.

† Fuller's ' Worthies,' *ante* p. 343 of vol. ii.

‡ The Bishop's Walk and the Bishop's Times, By Orwell. Cambridge : Macmillan and Co. 1861. The measure will reveal the source of earlier quotations in this memoir ; and certainly the gifted author promises to take a high place among the poets of Scotland. It may be noted here, that among the few Puritan books in the library of Leighton (preserved at Dunblane) are Sibbes's Bruised Reed (6th edition, 1638) and Soul's Conflict (4th edition, 1638).

Two hundred years have come and gone,
Since that fine spirit mused alone
On the dim walk, with faint green shade
By the light-quivering ash-leaves made,
    And saw the sun go down
    Beyond the mountains brown.

Slow pacing with a lowly-look,
Or gazing on the lettered book
Of Tauler, or A Kempis, or
Meek Herbert with his dulcimer,
    In quaintly pious vein
    Rehearsing a deep strain:

Or in the Gold-mouthed Greek he read
High rhetoric, or what was said
Of Augustine's experience,
Or of the Gospel's grand defence
    Before assembled lords,
    In Luther's battle-words.

Slow-pacing, with a downcast eye,
Which yet, in rapt devotion high,
Sometimes its great dark orb would lift,
And pierced the veil, and caught the swift
    Glance of an angel's wing,
    That of the Lamb did sing;

And with the fine pale shadow, wrought
Upon his cheek by years of thought,
And lines of weariness and pain,
And looks that long for home again;
    So went he to and fro
    With step infirm and slow.

A frail, slight form—no temple he,
Grand, for abode of Deity;
Rather a bush, inflamed with grace,
And trembling in a desert place,
    And unconsumed with fire,
    Though burning high and higher.

A frail, slight form, and pale with care,
And paler from the raven hair
That folded from a forehead free
Godlike of breadth and majesty—
    A brow of thought supreme
    And mystic, glorious dream.

And over all that noble face
Lay somewhat of soft pensiveness
In a fine golden haze of thought,
That seemed to waver light, and float
    This way and that way still,
    With no firm bent of will.

God made him beautiful, to be
Drawn to all beauty tenderly,
And conscious of all beauty, whether
In things of earth or heaven or neither;
    So to rude men he seemed
    Often as one that dreamed.

But true it was that, in his soul,
The needle pointed to the pole,
Yet trembled as it pointed, still
Conscious alike of good and ill;
    In his infirmity
    Looking, O Lord, to thee.

Beautiful spirit! fallen, alas,
On times when little beauty was;
Still seeking peace amid the strife,
Still working, weary of thy life,
    Toiling in holy love,
    Panting for heaven above:

I mark thee, in an evil day,
Alone upon a lonely way;
More sad-companionless thy fate,
Thy heart more truly desolate,
    Than even the misty glen
    Of persecuted men.

    For none so lone on earth as he
    Whose way of thought is high and free
    Beyond the mist, beyond the cloud,
    Beyond the clamour of the crowd,
        Moving, where Jesus trod,
        In the lone walk with God.

We have here the very man before us, and the very books he loved, and the very age he 'fell on,' and from which he was 'taken away.' Looking at the portrait, over and over engraved for the early quartos and duodecimos, and his one folio, Richard Sibbes must have been a man of larger mould, of more massive head, ampler brain-chamber, keener vision than Robert Leighton.* As

---

* Russell, in his 'Memorials of Fuller' (1844), and Mr Mayor, in his prefatory remarks to Catlin's MS., from the Baker MSS., have anticipated the comparison of Sibbes with Leighton. The former says—'Dr Richard Sibbes . . . a writer surpassed by none in that purity and depth of true spirituality, which also characterised

one studies the ruff-girted 'Master'-capped face, a more robust soul looks out from the benignant eyes. The seamed and lined forehead tells of deeper thinking, not without storms of doubt and wrestling (that always *so* leave their mark, like the waves on the sea-shore sands, as though the soul's mystic sea beat there). But the 'inner men,' in their spiritual-mindedness, unworldliness, meekness, humility, peacefulness, surely very closely resemble one another.

But now the stage darkens for 'the end,'

'Like a cave's shadow enter'd at mid-day.' *

He has to preach but other two 'sermons,' and then go forth on the last great journey. With strange fitness he chooses for his texts, John xiv. 1, 2, 'Let not your heart be troubled ; ye believe in God, believe also in me. In my Father's house are many mansions; it it were not so, I would have told you.'

CHAPTER XII.

'THE VALLEY OF THE SHADOW OF DEATH.'

Last Illness—Finishes ' The Soul's Conflict'—Draws up his ' Will '—
'Falls on Sleep.'

Having preached the last of these two 'sermons,' he 'fell sick that very night, June 28,' with some un-named illness. Feeling that he was indeed dying, he, on ' July 1,' put the finishing touches to his 'Address to the Christian Reader,' for the 'Soul's Conflict,' which had been passing through the press during his absence at Cambridge. Glancing over the proof-sheets, he detected certain passages which he found misunderstood, and noticed them ; but apparently was too weak to do more. On the 4th, he ' set his house in order,' by revising and altering his ' last will and testament.' He had many friends, gentle and simple, and it is with no common satisfaction that it is in our power to present this closing memorial :—†

Leighton in a succeeding age,' p. 81. The latter—' When we consider the beauty of Sibbes' language, and the gentleness of his temper, in both which respects he almost deserves the name of the Puritan Leighton, we cannot but wonder at the general neglect which has obscured his memory,' p. 253.

* 'Adon :' Poems. By Mrs Clive. 1856. P. 39.

† Extracted from the Principal Registry of Her Majesty's Court of Probate, in the Prerogative Court of Canterbury.

'In the name of God, amen, I, Richard Sibbs, Doctor of Divinity, weake in body, but of p'fect memory, doe make and ordaine this my last will and testament, in manner and forme followeing: First, I comend and bequeath my soule into the hands of my gratious Saviour, whoe hath redeemed it wth his most pretious blood, and appeares now in heaven to receave it, with humble thankes that he hath vouchsafed I should be borne and live in the best tymes of the gospell, and have my interest in the comforte of it; as alsoe, that he hath vouchsafed me the honour of being a publisher thereof wth some measure of faythfullnes. My body I would have to be buried at the discretion of my executors. And as for that outward estate that God. in his rich goodnes, hath blessed me w^thall, my minde and will is as followeth: First, I give and bequeath unto my brother Thomas Sibbs of Thurston, in the countie of Suffolk,* all my messuages, lands, and tenements, with the appurtenances, lyeing and being in Thurston aforesaid, or elsewhere, for and dureing the terme of his naturall life; and after my said brother's decease, to John Sibbs, sonne of my late brother John Sibbs, and now a student at Katherine Hall, in Cambridge,† and to his heires for ever: Item, I give unto my sister, Margaret Mason, fourtie pounds; and unto the children of my late sister, Susann Lopham, deceased, the some of thirty pounds, to be equally devided amongst them; as likewise, I give unto the children of my late sister, Elizabeth King, deceased, the some of fourtie pounds, to be equally devided amongst them; the said threescore and ten pounds, soe given to the children of my said sisters, I would have payed to the said children, severally and proporconably, at the dayes of their marriage, or when they shall accomplish their severall ages of one-and-twenty yeares, or otherwise sooner, at the discretion of my executors: Item, I give unto my uncle Sibbs, yf he be liveing, fourtie shillings; and unto the children of my late aunte . . . . . who dwelt in or neer Waldingfeild, in Essex,‡ the some of three pounds: Item, I give unto my cosen, Jeremy Huske, unto my cosins, Anne Beckett and Elizabeth Beckett, to every of them fourtie shillings: Item, I give unto the poore of the said towne of Thurston twentie shillings: Item, I give unto such of my poore kindred as are now dwelling at Stowlangton,§ in Suffolke, or elsewhere, whoe are now knowne to my executors, fourtie shillings, to be disposed according to the discretion of my executors: Item, I give unto James Joyner of London, whoe hath beene very faithfull in his service unto me tenn pounds; and to my loveing frends, Mr Dermer, haberdasher, dwelling on Ludgate Hill, twenty shillings, and to his wife twentie shillings, and to Widdow Dermer twentie shillings; and to my good friends Goodman Pinkaur and Goodman Rocke, dwelling in Perpoole Lane, to each of them twenty shillings: Item, I give unto Mr Nicholas Parry, steward of Grayes Inne, three pounds; and to Mr Guy, cheife cooke there, a ring of tenn shillings; and to his under servants, to be disposed at his discretion, the some of twenty shillings in the whole: Item, I give unto the three cheife butlers of Grayes Inne, to every of them, twenty shillings; alsoe, I give unto the inferiour servants of that house twenty shillings, to be disposed of according to the discretion of the steward; and as for that Hono^ble Society of Grayes Inne, I have nothing to bequeath unto it but the prayers of a sicke and dyeing man, that it may continue to be still a semenary of worthy men,

---

* See B in Appendix to this Memoir.   † *Ibid.*
‡ This is a slip. It is in Suffolk, near Sudbury, on borders of Essex.
§ Stowlangtoft, three miles from Thurston.

whoe may be alwayes ready to maintaine religion and justice, wth humble thankes for all their kindnesse and loveing respects towardes mee: Item, I give unto my auncient and deare frend, ould Mr Mew, in remembrance of my love, one of Mr Downham's books, called a Direccon to a Christian Life;* and to my deare and very worthy frend, Mr John Pym,† a ring of fourtie shillings: Item, I give unto my very good frend, Mr William Mew, one silver spoone, now in the custody of James Joyner aforenamed: Item, I give unto the poore of the parrish where I shal be buried twenty shillings: Item, I give unto my very worthy, religious, and bountifull frend, Mrs Mary Moore,‡ as a poore remembrance of my harty love unto her, one ryng of fourtie shillings; and to my very worthy frends Sr Robert Brooke of Langly, to his lady,§ and to his brother, Mr John Brooke, to each of them a ring of fourtie shillings; and to my kind frend, Mr Stevens of Gloucester-shire, a ring‖ of twentie shillings; and to my worthy friend, Mr Capell, ¶ late preacher in Gloucestershire, twenty shillings: Item, I give five pounds to the poore of the p'ishes of Trinity and St Andrews, in Cambridge: Item, Whereas there is due unto me, from the Colledge of St Katherine, in Cambridge, one hundred pounds, for wch Mr Goodwyn and Mr Arrow Smith** stand bound to mee, haveing the seale of the said colledge for their securetie, I doe hereby give and bequeath unto the said colledge, for ever, the said some of one hundred pounds, for the setling of a scholarship of fower pounds p. ann.; to wch said schollership my will and desire is, that my kinsman, John Sibbs, aforemenconed, shal be first elected and admitted; and that in all future eleccons, when the same shal be void in tyme to come, yf any of my kindred shal be then students in the said colledge, the p'son soe of kynne to me shal be p'ferred before another: Item, I give unto my loveing frend, Mr Catline, preacher of Thurston, fourtie shillings: Item, I give unto my good frend, Mr Almond of Cambridge, fyve pounds, praying him to im-ploy the same for the benefit of his sonne and my godsonne: Item, I give unto my godsonne, Richard Clerk, fortie shillings; and whereas, by the will of Mrs Gardiner, late of London, widdow, deceased, I was desired to dispose a certain some of money, in such manner as in her said will is spe-cified, all wch money hath beene accordingly disposed, excepting only fyve pounds, payable unto Mr Symons of Katherine Hall, my will is therefore is that payment be made of the said fyve pounds unto Mr Symonds afore-said; and to my reverend frende, Dr Gouge, I doe give, as a testimony of my love, twenty shillings, desiring him to take the paynes to preach my funerall sermon:†† Item, My will is, that my reverend frend, Mr Downeham, shall have two of those bookes of his owne making backe againe wch were by him delivered unto me, and are remayning in my studie at Grayes Inne; all the rest of my goods and chattles, my funerall, debts, and legacies being payed and discharged, I give unto my brother and kinsman before named— that is to saie, to my brother Thomas Sibbs, and my nephew John Sibbs, formerly menconed, whome, together wth John Godbold of Grayes Inne,

---

* Published 1622, and entitled 'A Guide to Godliness; or, a Treatise of a Chris-tian Life.' The author was John Downame or Downham, B.D., brother of George, Bishop of Derry. He died 1644.

† See references in loc. at p. cxxxvii, Appendix A

‡ Sibbes dedicates Culverwell's 'Time Well-spent' to her, ante p. xciii, seq.

§ See reference in loc. p. cxxxvii, Appendix A.

‖ Ibid.   ¶ Ibid.   ** Drs Goodwin and Arrowsmith.

†† See Mr Mayor's note in loc.   Appendix A.

Esquire, I doe hereby ordayne, constitute, and appoynt to be the executors of this my last will and testament, giving unto the said Mr Godbould a peece of my owne plate, such as himself shall choose out of that plate of myne, which is now in the custody of the said James Joyner; and I doe entreate my worthy and very loveing frends, Sʳ Nathaniel Rich, Sir Nathaniell Barnardiston,* and Sʳ William Spring, Knighte,† to be overseers of this my will, desireing my executors, in all things of difficulty, to be advised by them in the execution of the same; and as a remembrance of my love to every of the said overseers of my will, I give unto each of them a ring of twentie shillings.—In wittnes whereof I have hereunto set my hand and seale, this fourth daye of July, in the eleaventh yeare of the raigne of our sov'aigne Lord Charles, by the grace of God, kinge of England, Scotland, France, and Ireland, defender of the faith, &c., and in the yeare of our Lord God 1635. Signed, sealed, and published to be the last will and testament of the said Richard Sibbs in the presence of us.

PROBATUM fuit testamentum supʳscriptum apud London coram venᵘ viro magistro Willimo Merricke legum doctore: Surrogato venˡⁱˢ viri Domini Henrici Marten militis, legum etiam doctoris, curiæ prerogativæ Cantuar. magistri, custodis sive comʳⁱⁱ legitime constituti; undecimo die mensis Julii anno Domini millesimo sexcentesimo tricesimo quinto, Juramentis Thomæ Sibbs et Johannis Sibbs duorum executorum in senior ‡ testamento nominatorum: Quibus commissa fuit administracio omnium et singulorum bonorum piriu (?) et creditorum dicti defuncti de bene et fideliter administrando eadem ad sancta dei evangelia juratis: Reservata potestate similem commissionem faciendi Johanni Godbould Ar: alteri executori etiam in senior ‡ testamento nominato cum ven'it eandᵐ petitum.'

His will was drawn up on Saturday the 4th, and then he quietly waited his 'change.' '*Paulisper O senex, oculos claude, nam statim lumen Dei videbis*' ('Shut thine eyes a little, old man, and immediately thou shalt see the light of God'§).

Thus remembering his kinsmen and friends left behind, even the humblest, and looking UPWARD, he 'WALKED THROUGH the valley of the shadow of death,' and went, from the Sabbath below (*it was a Sabbath morning*) to the Sabbath above, to 'be with the Lord.' 'Blessed are the dead who die in the LORD. . . . Yea, saith THE SPIRIT, for they rest from their labours, *and their works do follow them*,' Rev. xiv. 13. He died 5th July 1635, in the 58th year of his age. An entry in the 'Register' of St Andrew's Church, Holborn (within which parish Gray's Inn is situate), tells us he was buried there on the next day:—

* Sir Nathaniel Barnardiston. The 'Rich' and 'Barnardiston' families are historic in their warm support of the Puritans. It were superfluous to annotate names that are found in every Puritan 'History.'

† Sir William Spring, Knt. He was of Pakenham, near Bury St Edmunds, of the ancient family of Lavenham. See Burke's 'Extinct' Baronetcies; also *ante* page xxvi.

‡ Qu. 'superscripts?'—ED.

§ Sozomen, lib. ii. cap. ii. Stanford's Alleine, p. 21.

'1635. July 6. Richard Sibbes, D.D., sometime preacher in Gray's Inn, died in his chambers at Gray's Inn, 5th.' *

1.

'Servant of God! well done;
Rest from thy loved employ;
The battle fought, the victory won,
Enter thy Master's joy.'
—The voice at midnight came;
He started up to hear:
A mortal arrow pierced his frame.
He fell,—but felt no fear.

2.

Tranquil amid alarms,
It found him in the field,
A veteran slumbering on his arms,
Beneath his red-cross shield:
His sword was in his hand,
Still warm with recent fight,
Ready that moment at command,
Through rock and steel to smite.

3.

The pains of death are past,
Labour and sorrow cease,
And life's long warfare closed at last,
His soul is found in peace.
Soldier of Christ! well done;
Praise be thy new employ;
And while eternal ages run
Rest in thy Saviour's joy. †

I would have my readers turn to the perhaps over-garrulous, yet interesting 'reflections' upon the death of Sibbes,‡ and add only a few words by Ashe, Church, and Nalton:—

'This bright star, who sometimes with his light refreshed the souls of many of God's people while he shone on the horizon of our church, set, as we say, *between the evening of many shadows and the morning of a bright hoped-for reformation*, which, though for the present (1654) overcast, yet being so agreeable to the mind of Jesus Christ, and ushered in with the groans and prayers of so many of his saints, we doubt not but will in God's own time break forth gloriously, to the dissipating of those clouds and fogs which at the present do eclipse and darken it.' §   Even so:—

'God's saints are shining lights; . . . .
They are indeed as pillar-fires,
Seen as we go;
They are that city's shining spires
We travel to.' ‖

A. B. G.

* It has been found impossible to identify his grave; no stone, the simplest, marks it. Is there to be no memorial raised?

† James Montgomery, 'The Christian Soldier.' Poetical Works, p. 305, ed. 1 vol. 8vo. 1851.

‡ Appendix A, p. cxxxviii, *seq.* See also B, pp. cxl–xli, in Appendix, for notices of Sibbes's family and name; and C, p. cxli, for references concerning his successors at Gray's Inn and Catharine Hall

§ 'To the Reader,' Heav. Conf. between Christ and Mary, 12mo. 1654.

‖ Vaughan, as *ante* p. 39.

APPENDIX TO MEMOIR.

A, page xxvi, *et alibi.*—ZACHARY CATLIN.

It has been 'deemed proper to give in full, in this appendix, the 'Memoir' of Sibbes, drawn up by Zachary Catlin (the manuscript of which, as has been stated, is in my possession). Accordingly it is subjoined, *verbatim et literatim* from the original holograph with signature. Two copies of this 'Memoir' are preserved at Cambridge; one among the Baker MSS. (xxxviii. 441–446); the other, recently presented, in University Library.* That by Baker has been edited with scrupulous fidelity by Rev. J. E. B. Mayor, M.A.; and forms one of the 'Communications' of the Cambridge Antiquarian Society (read December 1. 1856, No. vii. pp 252–264). It is to be regretted that it abounds with the most singular misreadings; for which Baker, not Mr Mayor, must be held responsible. Mr Mayor's notes, characteristically full of out-of-the-way reading, are appended. They are marked M. That in University Library, Mr Cooper informs me, 'is a transcript written about 1750, and contains some slight verbal variations from the Baker MS.,' but he 'adds, ' these variations can be of little value, because the scribe read the olden hand so imperfectly, that he throughout calls the subject of the memoir " Gibbs." '

Of Catlin very little is known beyond the incidental notices of himself and father, in his memoir of Sibbes. The 'Diary of John Rous, incumbent of Santon Downham, Suffolk, from 1625 to 1642, edited by Mary A. E. Green, (Camden Society, 4to, 1856,)' introduces him thus :—

'Upon Shrovemoonday, February 13. [A.D. 1632], Mr Catlin preaching at Bury, gave out before his sermon that it was good the ministers of the combination wold meete to consulte of the making of the combination, that those ministers that wold doe good might be put in seasonably for it. I learned since, that a newe-come minister was put in first in the combination, to beginne on Plough Moonday, but as it seemed would not goe before the graver preachers, and, therefore, lefte the day unprovided; but Mr Catlin by entreaty, preached at that time, *ex improviso*, and after wold have beene freed of this his owne time, but could not (thus he said before the sermon), and in his sermon said thus much obiter, which I heard. We are blamed for our churches, but it is certaine, that these courtes extracte more from us than will repayer our churches, adorne them, and keepe them so.' Pp. 68, 69.

Thirston.— Mr Catlin's sermon.

* A third is in Harl. MSS., 6087, fol. 17.

Mr Mayor has overlooked the marginal-note, ' Thirston,' when he asks if our Zachary Catlin were ' the Mr Catlin mentioned by John Rous.' ' Thirston,' *i.e.*, Thurston, gives the answer in the affirmative. Mr Cooper has favoured me with a note of various Catlins of the several colleges, Cambridge. There is a Zachary Catlin of Christ's, B.A. 1598, M.A. 1602. This was probably our Zachary. There is a Jonathan Catlin of Catharine-Hall, B.A. 1631, M.A. 1635, who was most likely the son mentioned as cared for by Sibbes.

The name, spelled ' Catling' and ' Catlyn,' occurs in Mr Bright's volume (*ante* page cxxi), as an 'overseer' in the will of one of the Nether-hall Brights, and elsewhere as a ' witness ' (see pp. 108, 128). I have been unable to trace to any library the two sermons published by him (*ante* page cxxiii). Considerable ' Notes ' on the family and name of Catelyne or Catlin (unpublished), will be found in ' Davy's Suffolk Collections,' vol. xlvi. (pp. 312–24). . . . Pedigrees C, Caa—Cha ; Mus. Brit. Jure Emptionis, 19, 122. Plut. clxxvi. E. With these slight memoranda, I beg now to submit, ' Dr Sibbs, his Life, by Zachary Catlin.'

At the Request of a Noble Friend, S[ir] W. Spring,[*] I haue here willingly contributed to the happy memory of that worthy man of God Doctour Sibs a few such Flowers, as I could collect, eyther from the certain Relation of those yt knew his first Education, or from mine own observation of him, at that distance, whereat we lived. And if any thing here recorded,
Mr Clark of may seem convenient for His purpose, who is (as I am in-
London.[†] formed) about to publish the Lives [‡] of some Worthyes lately deceased, I shall think my labour well bestow'd. For I am not of that Philosopher's mind, who lighting upon a Book newly put forth, entitled, The encomium of Hercules, cast it away, saying, Et quis Lacedæmoniorum eum vituperavit ? accounting it a needles [§] work to prayse him, whom noe man did, or could find fault withal. I rather iudge it a commendable thing, to perpetuate and keep Fresh the Memory of such worthy men, whose examples may be of use, for Imitation, in this declining, and degenerate Age. But I come to the matter.
He was born This Richard, the eldest Son of Paul Sibs and Johan, was
5 77. born at Tostock‖ in Suffolk, 4 miles from Bury, anno domini 1577, from whence his Parents soon removed, to a Town adioining, called, Thurston, where they lived in honest Repute, brought up, and maried divers children, purchased some Houses and Lands, and there they both Deceased. His Father was by his Trade, a Wheelewright, a skilful and painful workman, and a good sound harted Christian. This Richard he brought up to Learning, at the Grammar Schole, though very ¶ unwillingly, in regard of the charge, had not the youth's strong Inclination to his Book, and wel profiting therein, with some Importunity of Freinds prevailed so far, as to continue him at Schole, til he was fit for Cambridge. Concerning his
His industry loue to his Book, and his Industry in study, I cannot omit the
in his study. Testimony of Mr. Thomas Clark, High Constable, who was

---

[*] See Prynne's ' Canterb. Doome,' p. 376.—M.
[†] Mr Clark of London. Probably ' Samuel Clarke,' who included a Memoir of Sibbes in his ' Thirty-two lives ' (*ante* p. xxxvii), without however using Catlin's MS. Perhaps as the volume was published in 1652, and the MS. is dated November 1st of that year, it may not have reached him in time. But neither does any trace of it appear in subsequent editions.—G.   [‡] ' Plan ' in Baker, by Mr Mayor.—G.
¿ ' Useless ' in Baker, by Mr Mayor. I designate the remaining mis-readings by M. B.—G.   ‖ ' Tastock ' in M. B.—G.   ¶ ' Yet ' in M. B.—G.

much of the same Age, and went to schole, together with him, at the same Time, wth one M^r. Rich. Brigs (afterward, Head Master of the Free Schole at Norwich) then teaching at Pakenham church. He hath often told me, that when the Boies were dismist from Schole, at the usuall Houres of eleuen, and 5, or 6, and the rest would fal to their pastime, and sometimes to plaiing the Waggs with him, being haimlet* and meanly apparel'd, for ye most part in Leather, it was this Youth's constant course, as soon as he could rid himself of their unpleasing company, to take out of his Pocket or Sachel, one Book or other, and so to goe reading† and meditating, til he came to his Father's house, wch was neere a mile of, and so as he went to Schole agen. This was his order also, when his Father sent him to the Free Schole at Bury, 3, or 4 Miles off, every day. Whereby ye said M^r. Clark, did then conceive yt he would in Time prove an excellent and Able man, who of a child was of such a manly staydnes § and indefatigable industry in his study. His Father at length grew weary of his expenses for books and learning, took him from Schole, bought him an Axe and some other tooles, and set him to his own Trade, to the great discontent of the youth, whose Genius wholy caried him another way. Whereupon, M^r. *Greaves* ‖ then Minister of Thurston, and M^r. Rushbrook an Attorney there, knowing the disposition and fitnes of the lad, sent him, without his Father's consent, to some of the Fellowes of S^t. John's colledge, of their acquaintance, with their Letters of Recommendation, where, upon examination, he was so wel approved off, that he was presently entertained as a Sub-sizar, shortly after chosen Scholer of the House, and at length came to be Fellow of ye Colledge,¶ and one of the Taskers of ye University, His Father being hardly brought to allow him 20 Nobles a yeare toward his maintenance in Cambr., to which some good friends in the country, M^r. *Greaves*,** M^r. Knewstub,†† and some others, made some addition, for a Time as need required.

ἰαν ἡ φιλ-ομαθης, ἰση πολυμαθης. Tis one signe of a scholar to be φιλόπονος. —Ascham.‡

His profiting in Cambr.

Anno domini 1608, I came to be Minister of Thurston, and he was then a Fellow of the Colledge, and a Preacher of good Note in Cambr., and wee‡‡ soon grew§§ wel acquainted, for whensoeuer he came down into ye Country, to visit his Mother and brethren (his Father being deceased) he would never faile to preach with us, ‖‖ on the Lords day, and for the most part, twice, telling me, that it was a work of charity, to help a constant and painful preacher, for so he was pleased to conceiue of me. And If there were a Communion appointed at any Time, he would be sure not to with-draw himselfe after sermon, but receiving the Bread and wine at my hands, he would always assist me in the distribution of ye cup to the congregation.

As for his kindnes to his kindred,¶¶ and neglect of the world, it was very remarkable, for this I can testify of my own know-ledge, that purchasing of M^r. Tho. Clark, and others in our Town, a Mesuage and Lands, at seueral times, to the value of fifty pounds per annum, he paid the Fines to the Lords, but never took one peny of the Rents or profits of them, but left the Benefit wholly to his

His kindnes to his kindred and his singular neglect of ye world.

---

* ' Humble ' in M. B.—G.   † ' Studying ' in M. B.—G.
‡ Not given in M. B.—G.   § ' Stryde ' in M. B.—G.   ‖ ' Gwinn ' in M. B.—G.
¶ ' That house ' in M. B.—G.   ** ' Graves ' in M. B—G.
†† See Brook's ' Puritans,'vol. ii. p. 308, *seq.* ; Clarke's ' Lives of Thirty-two Eng-lish Divines,' ed. 1677, p. 133 ; Geffrey Whitney's ' Emblems,' p. 223 ; Bancroft's ' Daungerous Positions,' pp. 5, 57 (Bk. 2, c. 10), 44 (Bk. 3, c. 2), 120, 122, 143 ; Sutcliffe's ' Answere to Throckmorton,' p. 47 ; Prynne's ' Canterb. Doome,' p. 376.—M.   ‡‡ ' Was ' in M. B.—G.   §§ ' Grown ' in M. B.—G.
‖‖ ' Me ' in M. B.—G.   ¶¶ ' Friends ' in M. B.—G.

Mother, and his 2 Brethren,* as long as he liued. So much did this Heavenly-minded Man of God slight this present world (which the most men are so loth to part withal, when they Dye) that he freely and undesired, parted with it, whilst he liued, requiring nothing of them, but only to be liberal to the poore. Nay ouer and besides, if any faithful honest man came down from Cambridge or London, where he liued, by whom he might conveniently send, he seldome or never fayled to send his Mother a Peice of Gold, for the most part, a ten shillings Piece, but 5 shillings was the least, and this he continued as long, as his Mother liued. And would she haue been persuaded to exchange her Country Life for the citty, he ofter told me, yt he would willingly have maintain'd her there, in good view and fashion, like his Mother, but she had no mind to alter her accustomed course of Life, in her old daies, contenting her self with her own Meanes, and that Addition, wch her Son made thereunto.

His special kindness to me. And for his special kindnes to my self, in particular, I cannot omit, that being Trusted by Personages of Quality, with diuers sumes of mony, for pious and charitable uses, he was pleased, among many others, not to forget Me. At one Time he sent me down three Twenty shillings peices of gold inclosed in a Letter : and at 2 other Times, deliver[ed] me, with his own hand, two Twenty shilling pieces His singular humility. more : and so far was this Humble Saint from Pharisaical ostentation, and vain glory, and from taking the honour of these good works to himself, that he plainly told me, that these Gratuities were not of his own cost, but being put in Trust, and † left to his own Discretion, in the distribution, he lookt upon Mee as One, that took great Paines in my ministry, and in teaching Scholers, and at that Time Labouring under the Burden of a great charge of children, and so thought me a fit object of their intended charity. And from myselfe His love descended down to my Son, for my sake, for whom ‡ (before he had euer seen him, being then at the Grammar Schole at Bury) he, then chosen M^r of Katherin Hal, promis'd me a Schollership there, of 5 pound a yeare, and to provide for His reality in his promises. Pollicitis dives quilibetis esse potest.§ him a Tutour and a chamber. And such was his constancy of spirit, and his Reality, that whatsoeuer promise he made me, he would be sure, both to Remember it, and to make it good, as freely as he first made it, that was, unaskt and undesired : and for these manyfold kindnesses, all that he desired at my hands, was no more but this, that I would be careful of the soules of my people, and in special of his Mother, his Brethren, and his sisters, and would give them good counsel, in their disposing themselves in Marriage, or upon any other occasion, as I saw, they stood in need. And this one thing, I may not passe over, concerning myself, that in his last wil and Testament, he gave me a Legacy of 40 sh. with the Title of his Loving Freind, wch I the rather mention, because I had not the least thought, to haue been in yt sort remembred by him, at his Death, liuing‖ at no lesse distance from him, then of three score miles. In a word, such was the Loueliness of this sweet ¶ seruant of God, such his learning, ʼparts, piety, prudence, humility, sincerity, Loue and meeknes of Spirit (whereof euery one was a Lodeston to attract unto, and fasten my spirit, close to his) that (I professe ingenuously) no man yt euer I was acquainted withal, got so far into my hart, or lay **

---

* ' Brothers ' in M. B., and so elsewhere. § Not in M. B.
† ' As ' in M. B.—G ‖ ' Being ' in M. B.—G.
‡ ' For whom ' dropped in M. B.—G. ¶ ' Same ' in M. B.—G.
** ' Was ' in M. B.—G.

so close therein: So that many Times I could not part from him, with dry eyes. But who am I? or what is it to be belov'd of me, especially for Him, that had so many and so great Friends, as he had? yet even to Me, the great God is pleased to say, My son give me thy Heart, Prov. 23 26. and this poor and contrite hart, I know, he wil not despise, Psal. 51. 17. And this Hart of mine, as small as it is, yet is too great, to close with a Proud, Profane, worldly, malicious hart, though it be in a Prince. But true* Vertue and Grace, are the Image of God himself, and where they are discerned† by Wisdom's children, they command the Hart, and are truly louely and venerable, whereas Carnal, vitious, and unmortified Affections (whereof this Man of God, was as Free, as any man, I know liuing) they do render a man (whateuer he bee), if not hateful and contemptible, yet at least less louely and honourable. But my Love to this good Man hath transported me beyond my purpose, wᶜʰ was to speake of some things, lesse visible to others, especially concerning his first Education: for when he came to the University and the Citty, there his Life, and Actions were upon a publick Theatre, and his own works, without a Trumpet, Prov. 31. 31 would prayse him in the Gates. As for his kindnes to his and 23. kindred, and to my selfe, I know none, yt took more notice of them, then I, and therefore I could not hide them from the His death world (upon this occasion) without some kind of Sacriledge. July 5th 1635 ætat 58.

But from his Life, I passe to his Death, and the disposing of his worldly estate, wherein are some things very Remarkable, and coming to my certain knowledge and observation, I neyther wil, nor dare‡ conceal them. His Death was some what soden; for having preach't at Graye's Inne, upon the Lords Day, on that sweet Text, Joh. xiv. 1, 2, 'Let not His Cygnea your Harts be troubled, ye belieue in God, Believe also in me. Cantio vel In my Father's House are many Mansions,' as if he had concio § presag'd his own Death, he fel sick that very night, and died on ye Tuesday‖ following, being the 5ᵗʰ of July A.D. 1635. Ætatis suæ 58, his Physitian, that knew his Body best¶ being then out of ye Citty; yet having his senses, and some respite of Time, as he set his Soule, so he set his His last will. House in order, revising his former will, and altering, what he thought fitt to be altered. And first, he Bequeathed and commended ** his Soule, into the hands of his gracious Saviour, who Redeemed it, with his most precious Blood, and appeared then in heaven, to receive it. He gave him humble thanks, that he had vouchsafed him, to be Note. born, and to live, in the Best Times of the Gospel, (mark this) and to have his Interest in the comfort of it. As also that he had vouch- safed him the Honour of being a Publisher of it, with some measure of Faithfulnes (mark this, you that contemne ye office of the ministry). His Body he ordered to be buried, at the pleasure of his Executors. And for his worldly estate, wherewith God had blessed him, he How he thus disposed of it. His House and Lands at Thurston, disposed his to the value of 50 lib. a year, or more, he gave to his young- lands and per- est and only Brother then liuing, Thomas Sibs, for ye terme sonal estate. of his natural Life, and the Remainder to John Sibs, the son of John, his second Brother deceased: and between these two, he diuided all his

* 'This' in M. B.—G.   † 'Discovered' in M. B.—G.   ‡ 'Doe' in M. B.—G.
§ This is the title given to Whitaker's last 'sermon,' published 1599, 4to.—G.
‖ This is a slip for Sunday. See Memoir, page cxxx., and title-page of 'last ser-
mons,' in this volume.—G.
¶ 'Best' in M. B.—G.   ** 'Committed' in M. B.—G.

personal estate, which clearly amounted to 650 lib. (his large Legacies, and funeral charges being discharged and satisfied) making them, ye exequestors of his Wil and Test⁴. To the children of his 3 sisters deceased he gave 110 lib. To other poore kindred 13 lib. To his faithful Servant, James Joynar, 10 lib. To other 5 in London, 5 lib. To the poore of the parishes of Trinity and S⁴ Andrew's in Cambridge, 5 lib. To the poore of the Parish of Thurston, and of the parish, where he should be buried, 2 lib. To the Steward of Grayes Inne, 3 lib. To the 3 cheife Butlars, 3 lib. To their Servants, 1 lib. To the chiefe Cook, a Ring of 10 sh. To his under Servants, 1 lib. To his deare and worthy Friend M⁴. Jo. Pym,* a Ring of 2 lib. To S⁴. Rob⁴ Brook† of Langley, his

Legacies given out 288 lib. 10 sh. Lady, and Brother, 3 Rings of 6 lib. To Mr. Stephens‡ a Ring of 2 lib. To M⁴ Capell,§ Preacher, 1 lib. To his loving friend Mr. Catlin, Preacher of Thurston, 2 lib. To Mr. Almond of Cambr. for his Son (ye Doctours Godson), 5 lib. To his Godson Rich⁴ Clark, 2 lib. To Mr. Gouge ‖ of London, whom he requested to preach at his Funeral, 1 lib.¶ To S⁴ Nath. Rich ;** to S⁴ Nath. Barnardistòn ;††and to S⁴ W⁴ Spring, Supervisors of his will, 3 Rings of 3 lib. To M⁴ Mary Moore, a Ring of 2 lib. To Mr. Jo. Godbold of Gray's Inn Esq., one of ye exequatours of his Will, the best peice of plate he had, valued at 10 lib. To Katherin-Hal in Cambr, for the setling of a Scholarship of 4 lib. per annum for ever, 100 lib. All ᵥich Legacies amount to the total summe of 288 lib. 10 sh.

His enlarging Katherin Hal. During the Time yt he was M⁴. of Kath-Hal, he was the Meane by his great friends, of buying in the Inne, adioininge ye Colledge, called The Bull, and so of enlarging the Buildings of the Colledge, to the value of 500 lib. as I am informed : But I leave this to ‡‡ a *melius Inquirendum*. O what a Pious and charitable disposition do these things discouer, in this precious Saint, to be had in everlasting Remembrance.

---

* Besides the common sources for Pym's life, consult the ' Charisteria and Epist Eucharist.' of Degory Whear, his tutor and acquaintance of many years' standing. ' Charist.' Dedn. and pp. 101, 102; ' Epist. Eucharist.' Nos. 21—28. Pym was a friend and connection of Brownrigg's. B's ' Life,' pp. 190, 191.—M.

† Sir Robert Brook of Langley, his Lady . . . . See ' Dedication ' of ' Fountain Sealed ' (*ante* page cxix)—G.

‡ Dr Stephens, editor of ' Statius,' Master of Bury ? ' Life of Isaac Milles,' 1721, pp. 8–12, 74.—M.

§ Richard Capel, Wood's ' Athenæ,' ed. Bliss, iii. 421, Clark's ' Lives' (as above), p. 303 *seq*.—M.

‖ Dr Wm. Gouge. See his life in Clark (as above), p. 234 *seq*., Harwood's ' Alumni Etonenses,' p. 202, Wm. Lilly's ' Life,' ed. 1774, p. 29, Prynne's ' Canterb. Doome,' p. 362, Life of Row ' in Clark's ' Lives of Eminent Persons,' (1683), pt. ii. p. 106, Brook's ' Lives of the Puritans,' iii. 165, *seq*.—M. Also ' Memoir' prefixed to his Exposition of ' Hebrewes,' folio, 1655, vol. i.—G.

¶ From a tract bound in the volume marked R. 10. 16 in the University Library of Cambridge (p. 525) it appears that 10s. was commonly charged to the poor, and 20s. to the rich, for a funeral sermon. The tract contains the answer of George Finch (a Cambridge man, brother to Lord Finch) to the articles against him A.D. 1641.—M.

** See Birch's James I., vol. ii., p. 55, and Whear's ' Charisteria,' p. 127.—M.

†† See his life in Clarke's ' Lives of Eminent Persons,' (1683), pt. ii., p. 105, *seq*. Cf. *ibid*. pp. 161, 163, 169, 172, 175 ; Calamy's ' Account,' pp. 636, 637 ; ' Contin.' p. 786.—M.

‡‡ The Black Bull was given by will to Cath. Hall by Dr Gostlin, for the founding of six scholars, &c.—M.

I shal conclude with an Observation, wch I made of the Time, when this holy man, and some other Godly and precious Divines, were taken out of this world, by the wise Providence of God. Tis that of ye Prophet Is : 57, I. That Righteous and merciful men are taken away, from the Evill to come. They enter into Peace, and rest in their Graues, as in Beds of Sleep. Thus ye Lord said, concerning good Josia, I wil gather thee to the Fathers, and thou shalt go to thy Grave in Peace, And thine eyes shall not see all ye Evil, wch I wil bring upon this place. In like manner, the Lord took away, about the same Time, with this Reverend man diuers, that their eyes might not see that great Evils, then ready to break out, upon these 3 kingdoms. To instance in some few, Dr. Sibs died July 5, 1635 ; Mr. Sam. Ward,* that Worthy Preacher of Ipswich, was censured in the High commission, and silencet in October follow^{s} ye same yeare 1635, and died, as I remember 1638. The Irish Rebellion, the slaughter of 100,000 Protestants in a yeare, the long, fatal war, between the King and Parl^{t}.

The time of his death. Isa. 57, 1.

2 K. 22. 19, 20.

Dr Sibs, Mr Sam. Ward.

Mr. Rogers† also, that Zealous and powerful Preacher of Dedham in Essex, died Octob: 15 : 1636. And I may not forget my own father also, Mr. Robert Catlin,‡ an aged and a faithfull Minister in Rutlandshire, about four score yeares old died July 24 : 1637: who Being unable any longer to serue his great Pastoral cure, he came over to Barham, neere Ipswich, to dy amongst his children (here) in Suffolk : who lying on his sick Bed, heard Mr. Fenton, a Minister relating the Heavy censure, that was then newly passed upon the Bishop of Lincoln, and Deane of Westminster, Doctour Williams, reputed at that Time a very good Man, whom my Father knew to be a great Freind to the Good ministers in his Diocese, and a great enimy to the setting the Tables Altarwise, and to the Altar worship, wch then began to be much advocated, and one that had done many munificent works of charity, and had given yearely a great summe to the Releife of the Lady Elizabeth. The Bishop, by the malice of Archbishop Laud and others his enemies, was suspended in the High Commission ab officio or beneficio, censured in the Star-Chamber, fined 10,000 lib. and cast into the Towre of London about July 15, 1637 : from whence he was fetchet out the beginning of this Parl^{t.} Nov. 3d, 1640, with great applause. My Father, I say, hearing of this Bishop's censure (wherein my Brother Wm. Catlin, a minister was deeply concerned, as being a witness for ye Bishop), He brake out into these words, before the 2 Ministers, and others then present in the chamber. Alas poore England, thou hast now seen thy best daies ; I that am 4 score yeares old, and I have in al my time seene no alteration in Religion, nor any foreign Enemy setting

Mr Rogers of Dedham.

Mr Robert Catlin.

Dr. Williams cast into ye Tower.

* See Brook's ' Lives of the Puritans,' vol. ii. p. 452, seq., with the authors there cited; also Heylin's 'Cyprianus Angl.' p. 120, seq.; Prynne's 'Canterb. Doome.' pp. 157, 159, 361, 375 ; Birch's 'James I.,' vol. ii. pp 226, 228, 232 ; Clark's 'Lives of Eminent Persons' (1683), pt. ii. pp. 154, 159 ; D'Ewes' 'Autobiography,' vol i. p. 249 ; Calamy's 'Account,' p. 636 —M. Also Mr Ryle's Memoir, prefixed to his 'Sermons' in present series (see Adams's, iii.).—G.

† See his life in Brook's 'Lives of the Puritans,' vol. ii. p. 421 : and Bastwick's 'Utter Routing,' p. 474, Prynne's 'Canterb. Doome,' pp. 363, 373, Calamy's 'Account,' p. 606, Clark's 'Lives of Eminent Persons' (1683), p. 64 (Life of Blackerby), Mather's 'Life of T. Hooker,' p. 8, Mather's 'Life of John Cotton,' pp. 24, 25.—M. Also Chester's 'John Rogers' . . . pages 245, seq. (1 vol. 8vo, 1861).—G.

‡ This account has been printed in Brook's 'Lives of the Puritans,' vol. ii. pp. 428, 429.—M.

foot in England, nor any Ciuil wars, amongst ourselves, do now forsee euil daies a comming. But I shal go to the grave in Peace. Blessed be that God, whom I have served, who hath accepted my weake service, and wil be mine exceeding great reward. And within a few houres, he departed this Life, and lies Buried in the Chauncell of the Parish Church at Barham, Doctour Young of Stow Market,* preaching at his Funeral : and as he Blessed God (with D^r· Sibs) yt he had lived in the best Times of the Gospel, so there was no great difference in the Time of their death. And shortly after the death of these men were those sparkles of discontent kindled between the Scots and us, wch were the sad Præludia, or beginnings of this late Universal Conflagration. The King went against the Scots, as far as York, in March 1638 : and the Scots were proclaimed Traitours in the Churches of England, in April following, and though this Proclamation were revoked, yet who knows not, what Tragical events have follow'd in al the 3 Kingdoms, to this very day,† to the astonishment of Heaven and Earth. This is ye very observation of Reverend Beza in his 70th Epistle : That as often as God kindleth and setteth vp these Lights (men of singular graces and special use in ye church) so often he testifies his good wil to y^ose Times and Places in a certen special and peculiar manner. But when he extinguishes these Lights and puts them out, it must be accounted as an evident testimony of his sore Displeasure. For (saith he) it is apparant in al Histories that when greivous Tempests are comming upon a People, The Lord is wont to withdraw his especial servants into the Haven beforehand, wch agrees with y^t of ye Prophet Isay 2. 2, 3, 5. Behold ye Lord wil take away out of Judah and Jerusalem ye Judges and ye Prophets ; the Wise man and ye Councellour and· ye Honourable : and the People shal bee oppressed one of another etc. And no marvel, for such men are the το κατεχος . . . meanes as a shield to keep off the wrath of God from the Places where they live. The Lord with held the Flood of waters from ye old world, til Noah was safely shut up in the Ark, and the very selfe same day (saith the Text) were the Fountaines of the Deep broken up and the windowes of Heaven opened. The Angel told Lot he could do nothing against wicked Sodom, till he was got out of that place. The Lord held off the king of Babilon from beseiging Jerusalem til good Josia was at rest. And ere the Roman Army sate down before it, the Lord by a Miracle warned the Christian Jewes to remove from thence to Pella. Again, no sooner was that worthy Bishop of Hippo St Augustin deceased, but the Citty was taken and sacked by the Goths and Vandals. No sooner was Martin Luther translated to a better Life, but the Smalcaldick warre brake out wch wasted almost al the Protestants in Germany. No sooner was that worthy man, aged Pareus taken from Heydelberg, but presently Marques Spinola with his Army entered the Town. And no sooner had the Lord taken away these worthy Divines, but presently the Fire of war and confusion (a iust punishment for our great and crying sins) brake out upon these 3 nations. For if the Foundations (of Religion and Government) be cast down and destroy'd, what can the Righteous do. The voice of wise men is not heard in the cry of Fooles : The counsel of moderate and unbiased men is not regarded in such a

Marginal notes: King went against ye Scots. March 1638. / Bezæ Ep. 70. / Gen. 7. 16. 11. 13. / Gen. 13. 22. 2 Chron. 34. 28, and 36. 6. / Josephus. / Augustine. / M. Luther. / D. Pareus. / Psal. 11. 3.

* The celebrated Scottish tutor and friend of John Milton.
† From 'very day,' on to 'The Lord in Mercy,' not in M.-B.—G.

Tempest of clamour, violence, and confusion. Such men would have been slighted and lay'd aside in such Times as these. The Lord therefore hath put them into their safe harbour and Haven of Rest, while wee that survive are tossed to and fro upon the turbulent Eurypus of Anabaptistical, Anarchical, Fanatical, and Atheistical barretings and Vittlitigations.*

The Lord in Mercy vouchsafe to stil the Raging of the waters, and the madnes of (that many headded monster) the People, that once more his faithful Servants in these 3 Nations, may enjoy a blessed calm. That there may yet once again, be Peace and Truth in our Daies. Lord save us, or we perish. Ps. 65. 7. Isay. 39. 8. Matt : 8. 25.

Compiled and attested, by Zachary Catlin, Minister of Thurston, Nov. 1. 1652: Anno ætatis 69 : currente.

(I have presented Catlin's MS. to ' University Library,' Cambridge).

B, pages xxix and cxxxi.—SIBBES'S FAMILY AND NAME.

The Will of Sibbes (*ante* p. cxxviii, *seq.*), enumerates various relatives deceased and alive. His father had died before 1608, and his mother, Catlin informs us, also predeceased him. Dr Sibbes himself never married, perhaps through the ' order ' of Gray's Inn, that forbad its ' preacher ' to marry. The name seems to have utterly died out, not in Suffolk merely, but everywhere. While all the other Puritans of this Series are living names, I have failed to trace any Sibbes beyond 1737. No doubt the blood has been transmitted in the issue of the several sisters named in the ' Will.'

The following *memorabilia* from the sources enumerated above each, contain all that I have been able to collect about the family and name.

I. Catharine-Hall ' Registers.'

(1.) John Sibbes, B.A. 1635 (mentioned in ' Will ').

(2.) Richard . . . B.A. 1664, M.A. 1668. (See entry in Thurston ' Register,' Mo. 2.)

(3.) Robert . . . B.A. 1675.

(4.) Richard . . . B.A. 1716.

II. Tostock ' Registers.'

The merest fragment of the ' Registers ' of Tostock has been preserved; and the first occurrence of the name of Sibbes therein, it will be observed, is long posterior to his death.

1. Hannah Sibbs, the daughter of Thomas Sibbs (probably a grand-nephew), and Elizabeth his wife, was baptized the 6th day of January 1679.

2. Francis, ye daughter of Thomas Sibbes and Elizabeth his wife, was baptized ye 5th of June 1683.

₊ See an entry from Thurston ' Register,' of her marriage.

3. Richard, the son of Thomas Sibbs and Elizabeth his wife, was baptized May ye 1st 1688.

From the ' deaths ' we find ' Thomas Sibbes was buried January ye 18th 1690,' and ' Elizabeth Sibbes, widow, was buried, August 9th 1706.'

4. John Nunn and Sarah Sibbes (probably a grand-neice), both of this parish, were married, April 12. 1697.

Of this marriage were born :—

(1.) Mary, ' baptized December ye 30th 1702.'

(2.) John, ' baptized January ye 9th 1706.' (Died in a few days.)

(3.) Esther, ' baptized May ye 26th 1708.'

* Qu. ' Vile litigations ?'—ED.

Of 'Sarah Sibbes' = Mrs Nunn, we read, 'Sarah, the wife of John Nunn of Thurston, was buried here, April 28th 1719.' A 'Frances Nunn of Rattlesden, was buried, Feb. 18. 1725.'

A third branch is as follows :—

5. 'John Limner of Chevington, and Elizabeth Sibbes (probably another grand-niece), of this town, were married, August ye 23d 1700.'

There was issue :—

'Esther, daughter of John Limner and Elizabeth his wife, . . baptized Octob. ye 15th 1701.'

III. Thurston 'Registers,' as Tostack.

Only two occurrences of the name of Sibbes are found :—

1. Titulus Matrimonii, 1707.

' Robert Steggles of Tostock, and Frances Sibbes of Thurston, married, Ap. 23.' (See under Tostock, No. 2.)

2. 'Mr Richard Sibbes, clerk, rector of Gedding 65 years, aged 93, Feb. 2. 1737.'

This was doubtless the 'Richard' of the Cambridge list (supra No. 2). He was probably non-resident. In the 'registers' of Gedding, only one entry during the whole period of his incumbency, bears his signature as ' rector.'

IV. Bright's ' Brights of Suffolk' (ante pp. lxxxv–vi).

In the family papers of ' the Netherhall Family,' John Sibbes, no doubt the Doctor's nephew, appears as a 'witness' in a dispute about a 'meadow' (page 127). On the back of a letter (January ye 6th 1703), is a memorandum by Thomas Bright, relating to accounts and rents, under the heads of Thurston, Pakenham, Barton, and Tostock, in which, among others, occur the names of ' John, Robert, and Thomas Sibbes,' perhaps 'tenants' on the estate. Finally, in a letter, 'June 10. 1729,' a Mr Howard writes to the famous beauty, ' Mary Bright,' that ' yesterday he view^d Mr Sibbs' copyhold lands, held of her manor.'

C, page cxxvi.—SUCCESSORS OF SIBBES IN HIS OFFICES.

1. ' PREACHER,' GRAY'S INN.

13th November 1635. Hannibal Potter, Dr of Divinity, chose preacher.

9th February 1641. Mr Jackson is chose lecturer, to preach twice of a Sunday.

28th May 1647. Mr Horton chose preacher.

13th January 1662. Mr Caley, preacher and lect^r of this Society, if he please to accept thereof.

12th November 1662. Mr Cradock chose lect^r, wth same allowance as Mr Wilkins.

2. ' MASTER,' CATHERINE HALL, CAMBRIDGE.

There was a keen contest for the ' Mastership.' The subsequently celebrated Bishop Brownrig was appointed. For interesting notice, with references, of Brownrig, and for the papers relating to the disputes, consult Mr Mayor's ' Autobiography of Matthew Robinson ' (pp. 130–146) ; also ' Garrard's Letter to Strafford (September 1. 1635, Strafford's Letters, vol. i. p. 462).

* 9 7 8 1 7 8 9 4 3 0 7 5 2 *